# Dancing in God's Love

by

Debi Barrington Merchant

*Published in the United States by: PenDragon Literary.*

*Cover Design: Annette Langevin Lewis*
*Author Photo: J.P. Brown*
*Interior Design: PenDragon Literary*
*Foreword: Pastor Ann Mann*



*ISBN: 978-0-9787833-2-7*

*Printed in the United States of America*

DANCING IN GOD'S LOVE

***This book is lovingly dedicated to:***

my daughter, Jeri Michelle Pace Brown (my first born)
and
my husband, Matthew Steven Merchant (2nd time was the charm)

May you both dance in God's love always.

## FOREWORD

Who doesn't need another friend? Debi invites us into her heart for a journey through the living Word of God. These daily devotions are more than simply reflections on scripture, they take us through one woman's walk with Jesus. And by taking us on that journey, Debi invites us into her life.

It has not always been an easy life. As she says, "divorce, death of a loved one, illness, murder, car wreck, moving, debt," have all been a part of her journey. And so, we sit with Debi, in a comfortable chair, sharing life's greatest tragedies and sweetest victories. And we cling to the One who gives us hope, our Lord and Savior Jesus Christ.

It was my privilege to serve as one of Debi's pastors at Due West United Methodist Church in Marietta, Georgia. One of my first memories of Debi was seeing her dancing in the church. Well, not really dancing. She was playing handbells with the handbell choir, and her feet had wings. I knew in that moment I needed to meet this woman who felt the Spirit of the Lord right down to her toes. And so we met. And we became fast friends. This book shows you why. She shares from her heart, with honesty and compassion. She is not perfect, and she shares that, too. And that is why she is so easy to love, and her devotions are so easy to read. So, come along, and meet your new friend Debi!

Blessings,
Pastor Ann

# INTRODUCTION

As I sit down to write this devotional book, I must admit that I don't know Hebrew, Greek, or Arabic. But I DO KNOW Jesus Christ. I know the Trinity – God the Father, God the Son, and God the Holy Spirit (or as I heard in a sermon once and prefer – God the Mother). I also know what the Scriptures herein have meant, and still mean, to me.

I in no way present myself as an expert on the Scripture, nor do I promote myself as perfect – I am far from it.

My daughter, Jeri, once asked me to share with her some of my favorite Scriptures. When I began to go through my Bible, I realized **how many verses** were actually my favorites. I emailed her several of them, but I realized later I didn't explain why they were favorites.

My goals with this book are: – 1) to enlarge the list of verses I emailed Jeri, and to share what they mean to me and why they are favorites, 2) to give busy people a quick, but meaningful moment with God each day of the year, and 3) to share with all y'all* why and how God is so important to me.

[*Author's Note: From time to time, I'll use brackets and/or parentheses to interject or explain something. I'm a Southern girl, with Southern roots and, as a result, Southern phrases. It's been said I write like I talk. For this book, that's perfect for me because I want it to come across as a conversation from your Southern friend, Debi, about what my Lord and His Word mean to me. ***Y'all*** means you all (or the plural of you), and ***all y'all*** is the plural form of y'all. Come to think of it, that may be redundant, but it's in my vocabulary so will probably pop up from time to time. I'll do my best to explain all the "Southern" phrases herein.]

The book is a compilation of my devotional journals beginning February 2008 to the present.

The majority of the verses will be from the New International Version (NIV), with occasional verses from other translations, as indicated.

In each case, the words I write will be what the passages have meant to me over the years of my faith journey. Occasionally, the same exact passage may show up on a different day with a different meaning – because on any given day we need to be open for something new from God. Various verses teaching me the messages I need in order to navigate life – different days; different verses; same Lord.

Even though I know God is a Spirit without gender, I refer to God using the male pronoun because to me He's my Heavenly Father.

As with any study of the Scripture, please take the time to read entire chapters to fully understand and grasp the context in which each passage was written. A lowercase a, b, c, etc. after a verse number means the first, middle, or end of the verse. Also, don't just read my words, start a Bible study journal of your own, as the Scripture speaks to you and opens your eyes to new blessings.

The evil in the world is beyond most of our comprehension because we are good people. Whether it hits you personally as it did my family in 2012, or whether it's the ripple effect of an assassination or mass murder, the evil feels like a choke hold on us. The only way I know to combat evil is to embrace God and dance in His love.

One of the biggest gifts we have is to be able to approach the living God with freedom and confidence, and yet many of us do not take advantage of that opportunity. We can do this any time, and when we neglect to do so we miss out on so much.

A review of my journals revealed several days I neglected to take advantage of this gift. I'm ashamed to admit it, but it wasn't until late 2016 that I got serious about *daily* devotions. Some of my reasons to miss were: "too busy", "too tired", "too much on my plate", "God knows I love Him, and I do pray for people daily, so what's the problem?"

The problem was I failed to open the most wonderful gift of all – time with my Lord! I'm sure God misses me when I don't spend time with Him, and I **know** how much I miss by **not** spending time with Him. It IS a choice.

May you feel the Presence of the Trinity, and may you accept the blessings into your life.

May we all realize the Gift, the price that was paid, and fall down at His throne and worship Him daily, Dancing in God's Love.

Debi Barrington Merchant

**Ephesians 3:12** (NIV) *In him and through faith in him we may approach God with freedom and confidence.*

January 1

**<u>2 Peter 3:8</u>** (NIV) *But do not forget this one thing, dear friends: With the Lord a day is like a thousand years, and a thousand years are like a day.*

This is a favorite verse because it helps me be patient when I feel God isn't working fast enough. It reminds me how important time is. A thousand years is a long time, for us, but a thousand years is just a wink for God.

I can relate to this in that I blinked, and the teenage girl I was at Hanahan High was a retiree from Federal Civil Service with over 34 years under her belt. I blinked and the 18-year-old who graduated in 1971, was 65 and on Medicare. I blinked, and the babies I had, were grownups with children of their own. I blinked, and our grand babies were teenagers. It's the same for all y'all. You blinked, and many years passed.

On this, the first day of a new year, let us realize we don't live one day at a time – we live one **<u>moment</u>** at a time. Make each moment count. Live with the eyes of your heart wide open, and the ears of your soul listening for God's still small voice. Happy New Year!

## January 2

**Matthew 6:25-26** (NIV) [25]*Therefore I tell you, do not worry about your life, what you will eat or drink; or about your body, what you will wear. Is not life more than food, and the body more than clothes?* [26]*Look at the birds of the air; they do not sow or reap or store away in barns, and yet your heavenly Father feeds them. Are you not much more valuable than they?*

This is a favorite because it is Jesus speaking right to us about God supplying our needs.

One day in mid-October 2010, I wrote in my devotional journal that I was convinced God would provide a way for me to cut back on my hours at a non-profit so I could do what He would have me do. Within days, things began to fall into place at the non-profit, and by the first day of March I was job sharing. I worked half the hours and half the responsibility. Much of the work I was responsible for could be done virtually, and not necessarily during business hours. I thought it was to pursue my writing, but God had other plans. Later that year a grandchild was born, and I was free to be the caregiver in lieu of a day care. And my summers were then free to also keep our grandchildren who were school age as well! What a gift this is for grandparents! Many memories were made during that special time.

God had a plan, and God opened a way. All I had to do was claim God's gift. Walking and talking with God through this journey we call life keeps us in tune with Him and His will for us. His will is never in opposition to what we are capable of doing, or what our heart's desire is. The key is being in sync with Him.

January 3

**2 Corinthians 4:16-18** (NIV) [16]*Therefore we do not lose heart, though outwardly we are wasting away, yet inwardly we are being renewed day by day.* [17]*For our light and momentary troubles are achieving for us an eternal glory that far outweighs them all.* [18]*So we fix our eyes not on what is seen, but on what is unseen. For what is seen is temporary, but what is unseen is eternal*

It's amazing to me how God speaks to us through His word. I first **really read** verse 16 on the insert of a Kutless* CD. It quickly became a favorite passage. One of the band members was honoring his dad, who was ill. I'm not sure, but I'm guessing he may have suffered from Alzheimer's like my daddy. After watching how that dreadful disease affects its victims, this is the perfect verse for those people of faith suffering from it or suffering along with loved ones who have it.

No matter what we are enduring on this earth, cling to our Source – God the Father, Son, and Holy Spirit. We WILL get through it, and we will do it with peace in our hearts. Can I get an amen?

*[*Christian band]*

January 4

**Psalm 5:2-3** (NIV) [2]*Listen to my cry for help. My King and my God, for to You I pray.* [3]*In the morning, O Lord, you hear my voice; in the morning I lay my requests before You and wait in expectation.*

Another favorite Psalm, this passage reminds me to seek God in the morning and set the tone for my day – my life. I realize there are times when a “first thing in the morning” visit with God just isn’t happening, but I know this for sure: when I’m able to begin my day with God, I have a better day. When we’re able to do that, we rest in His everlasting arms and He gives us peace and guidance. He destroys our enemies’ power over us. He gives us what we need for the day’s journey. It’s almost like He rides around on our shoulders, whispering in our ears. We hear His guidance, His peace, and His assurance. Hallelujah!!

January 5

**1 John 1:9** (NIV) *If we confess our sins, he is faithful and just and will forgive us our sins and purify us from all unrighteousness.*

I have been attending church since I was two weeks old. I have to admit, those early sermons are a bit fuzzy. Okay, full disclosure, I don't remember any of them. Suffice to say, trusting in God is the only life I know, and the only way for me to put one foot in front of the other. This is a favorite verse, because it affirms if I confess, He forgives, guides, and loves. He shines His Light on me, and His Peace is a blessing beyond measure. I drink it in and live! He purifies me, and I am humbled.

January 6

**<u>Luke 10:38-42</u>** (NIV) [38]*As Jesus and his disciples were on their way, he came to a village where a woman named Martha opened her home to him.* [39]*She had a sister called Mary, who sat at the Lord's feet listening to what he said.* [40]*But Martha was distracted by all the preparations that had to be made. She came to him and asked, "Lord, don't you care that my sister has left me to do the work by myself? Tell her to help me!"* [41]*"Martha, Martha," the Lord answered, "you are worried and upset about many things,* [42]*but few things are needed – indeed only one. Mary has chosen what is better, and it will not be taken away from her."*

These favorite verses remind me to focus on what's IMPORTANT, and THAT is something I need to be reminded of constantly! God implores us to meet Him early in the morning and stay with Him as Mary did. Martha was, as we Southerners are prone to say, "running around like a chicken with her head cut off"* getting all the things done, while Mary sat and learned at the feet of Christ. Even in our busy daily lives we have time for Christ if we make time. He's always there waiting with open arms for us to join Him.

[*It's a Southern thing – means *aimlessly.*]

January 7

**Psalm 42:1-2** (NIV) [1]*As the deer pants for streams of water, so my soul pants for you, my God.* [2]*My soul thirsts for God, for the living God. When can I go and meet with God?*

This is a favorite passage because the words beautifully depict how I sometimes feel in the midst of life's storms. My thirst and need for God are overpowering at those times, and once I visit with God, a peace comes over me like nothing else in this world. Several years ago, I was prone to have panic attacks. If you've ever experienced one, you know how scary they can be. My doctor at the time prescribed Xanax. I only took the medicine when I felt an attack coming on. As the years passed, I learned more and more to lean on God for my peace. I'm not saying you should stop taking your meds, I'm saying that, for me, I don't need them anymore. The Bible and prayer are my go-to's for panic attacks now, and they both work beautifully for me. Looking to God makes us radiant – He empowers us to meet our struggles head-on.

January 8

**Philippians 2:14-15** (NIV) [14]*Do everything without grumbling or arguing,* [15]*so that you may become blameless and pure, children of God without fault in a warped and crooked generation. Then you will shine among them like stars in the sky as you hold firmly to the word of life.*

This favorite passage is so pertinent in our times; so pertinent for me! I sometimes find myself griping and complaining about this or that, and usually for no good reason. There's no sense for me (or anyone) to be contrary for contrary's sake. Allowing God to help me navigate the things that grate on my last nerve keeps me focused on Him, and I would hope, shows all WHOSE I am. I'm a work in progress, but those who knew me when and those that know me now, can attest to God's influence. Right, family? Family? Y'all? "Just keep praying, just keep praying, just keep praying."

January 9

**John 10:27** (NIV) *My sheep listen to my voice; I know them, and they follow me.*

O, what joy, comfort and peace I feel when I read this favorite verse! Jesus spoke these words. He is our Shepherd, and He KNOWS us by name. Can you imagine?! We listen and follow Him. God takes bad situations and causes good to come out of them. **I'll never believe He causes** the bad things to happen. God wants good things for us. But I KNOW He takes the bad things and before we know it, something good is there. Something we may never have noticed without the storm. Can I get a witness?

January 10

**<u>Psalm 143:8</u>** (NIV) *Let the morning bring the word of your unfailing love, for I have put my trust in you. Show me the way I should go, for to you I entrust my life.*

God will help us every step of the way – we just have to ask, and he will direct us. I basically prayed Psalm 143:8 on a night in 2010 as I wrestled with how to help a family member with a major problem. I didn't realize it at the time, of course, but when I later read this verse, I was amazed at how King David and I felt the same way and prayed virtually the same prayer. That was a very humbling experience. My soul was in the exact same place. I thank God, our Father, for the Bible as relevant today as ever, and for leading me to favorite verses right at the moment I need them.

January 11

**2 Thessalonians 3:16** (NIV) *Now may the Lord of peace himself give you peace at all times and in every way. The Lord be with all of you.*

This favorite verse reminds me that true peace comes from God. I've spent so many years running around like a chicken with my head cut off [aimlessly, see January 6th] and left that Peace that Scripture promises out of my life. Praise God I began to change that in 2009, and continue to learn more each day about "letting go and letting God." How can we not trust the God of the Universe with our daily problems and tasks?! God created EVERYTHING! I'm pretty sure He knows how to help me prioritize my to-do-list – my life.

January 12

**<u>Ephesians 3:16-19</u>** (NIV) [16]*I pray that out of his glorious riches he may strengthen you with power through his Spirit in your inner being,* [17]*so that Christ may dwell in your hearts through faith. And I pray that you, being rooted and established in love,* [18]*may have power, together with all the Lord's holy people, to grasp how wide and long and high and deep is the love of Christ,* [19]*and to know this love that surpasses knowledge--that you may be filled to the measure of all the fullness of God.*

This passage is a favorite because it reminds me that God wants me to come and hear and internalize the breadth, depth, length, and height of His love. As we experience God's love for us on this level, we are able to share His love with others, not only verbally, but they will **SEE** the evidence of His Presence in our lives. We will radiate His love and His peace. I'm reminded that I might be the only experience of God's love that someone may see. It humbles me to know that I can and am used by God to spread His love. May I always do so, and when I fail to, may I repent and apologize to all I've hurt.

January 13

**Revelation 1:8 (KJV)** *I am Alpha and Omega, the beginning and the ending, saith the Lord, which is and which was, and which is to come, the Almighty.*

This favorite verse of mine just rolls off the tongue nicely, to me, in the King James Version (KJV) of the Bible. God is eternal – He was, He is, He will be. He will guide us, lead us, carry us – whatever is necessary to get us through whatever we are facing.

He cares about all things that we may deal with, small or large. Here are a some from my life – past, present, future:

- a lost cat (past) In my teens my cat was missing one Wednesday night before prayer meeting at church. I prayed for that silly cat to come home – he met us at the door as we drove into the carport.

- a dead iPhone battery (present) One night my cell phone wouldn't charge or sync. Pictures I hadn't downloaded to my laptop would be lost if I couldn't get it to work. I prayed and Googled it, on the verge of panic. But I didn't panic; I just turned it over to Him and went to bed. The next morning, I plugged it in, and heard the beautiful special sound it makes, as "This is the day the Lord has made" and "Be still and know that I AM God" scrolled across my phone as they do daily.

- a dependable God (future) Those verses will continue to greet me every morning on my iPhone, and my God will continue to walk with me always.

January 14

**Isaiah 40:28-31** (NIV) [28]*Do you not know? Have you not heard? The LORD is the everlasting God, the Creator of the ends of the earth. He will not grow tired or weary, and his understanding no one can fathom.* [29]*He gives strength to the weary and increases the power of the weak.* [30]*Even youths grow tired and weary, and young men stumble and fall;* [31]*but those who hope in the LORD will renew their strength. They will soar on wings like eagles; they will run and not grow weary; they will walk and not be faint.*

This is one of my all-time favorite passages. The first time I remember really embracing and understanding the words to this passage was early 1981. The new pastor that had recently come to our church was actually our age (let me just say that's when you begin to feel old), and the way he preached just opened up the Scriptures to me. I remember having my devotion on a Saturday evening (in the bathroom where young mothers must go for peace and quiet) and asking God to make these verses come alive for me. Can you believe the very next morning that was the sermon passage?! The pastor spoke of how God helps us over (soaring) our problems or through (walking or running) them. He also said we "faint not", because God carries us many times. WOW – the passage can't become more alive than that. Thank you, God.

January 15

**John 14:1** (NIV) *Do not let your hearts be troubled. You believe in God; believe also in me.*

Jesus is speaking these words to us today, just as He did centuries ago to the people who followed Him. This favorite verse brings me such comfort as it reminds me to trust God instead of worrying and fretting about the curve balls life throws at me. I also realized that the word *hearts* is plural, so this verse is meant for all people, y'all! The ones that were alive when Christ spoke the words, and all of us who have been born afterward. The Bible is as relevant today as when God whispered the words to the writers He chose.

January 16

**<u>Psalm 120:1 (KJV)</u>** *In my distress I cried unto the LORD, and he heard me.*

This has been a favorite verse of comfort to me since September 1973 when I received devastating news, and for the first time (there have been many times since) in my adult life screamed out at God. I actually held the Bible up toward the ceiling and screamed, “say something to me, Lord!” And then I sat down, and the Bible opened to this verse. Coincidence? NO! It was God speaking to a wounded and hurt child and reassuring that child that He was there and would ALWAYS be there for her… and He has been and still is. He is there for y’all, too!

January 17

**Psalm 121:1-2 (KJV)** [1]*I will lift up mine eyes unto the hills, from whence cometh my help.* [2]*My help cometh from the LORD, which made heaven and earth.*

As I continued reading that same night in September 1973, my eyes fell upon these verses as well because they were located on the same page in my Bible. These favorite verses give such imagery and a vision of lifting my eyes while in the depths and seeing the Light of God Who comforts me. How wonderfully cool is that? Can't you just imagine it? O, the depths of God's love! Can I get an amen?

January 18

**<u>Luke 12:15</u>** (NIV) *Then he said to them, "Watch out! Be on your guard against all kinds of greed; life does not consist in the abundance of possessions."*

Our lives are not what we have, but rather who we are and WHOSE we are. True followers of Christ are concerned for others and less concerned about possessions, money, or status in life. These favorite words of Jesus remind me to keep it real, and to know what's important. To know what truly matters and convey that to others with love in action. In this day (2021) and time, it seems ever more important to live the love we know and have through Christ.

January 19

**<u>Daniel 3:22-25</u>** (NIV) [22]*The king's command was so urgent and the furnace so hot that the flames of the fire killed the soldiers who took up Shadrach, Meshach and Abednego,* [23]*and these three men, firmly tied, fell into the blazing furnace.* [24]*Then King Nebuchadnezzar leaped to his feet in amazement and asked his advisers, "Weren't there three men that we tied up and threw into the fire?" They replied, "Certainly, Your Majesty."* [25]*He said, "Look! I see four men walking around in the fire, unbound and unharmed, and the fourth looks like a son of the gods."*

This passage is a favorite because, as was the case with Shadrach, Meshach, and Abednego, it assures me that God is with me no matter what I'm experiencing. I have felt Him with me many times through the trials that I have faced through the years. I know for a fact, without Him, I would not have made it. In the margin of my Bible, I've written: God is the game changer. He truly is. God gets right into that furnace we call life and walks with us!! (I was going to say, "how cool is that?", but I'm sure it would be hot, not cool...okay… I'll keep my day job. Oh, wait, I'm retired.)

January 20

**Romans 8:38-39** (NIV) [38]*For I am convinced that neither death nor life, neither angels nor demons, neither the present nor the future, nor any powers,* [39]*neither height nor depth, nor anything else in all creation, will be able to separate us from the love of God that is in Christ Jesus our Lord.*

No matter what circumstances I find myself in, these favorite verses give me strength. I refer to them as my Spiritual Pep Rally. Remember on game day in high school how we'd all come together in the gym for the pep rally to pump up the team for the game that night? Even if you hated football (I can't imagine why), you got all excited and pumped up. Please tell me high schools still do that! Anyway, these verses do the same thing the pep rallies on Friday did way back in high school. They touch my heart and get me all pumped up to go out and conquer whatever is attacking me.

January 21

**<u>Psalm 6:9</u>** (NIV) *The Lord has heard my cry for mercy; the Lord accepts my prayer.*

What a true comfort this favorite verse is to know that God IS listening to my prayers – even the ones I'm not sure how to pray. Even the ones where the answer might not be yes*. Even the ones when my heart is wrenching and hurting so badly, I can barely breathe. Yes, I've been there, done that. So has God. Remember Christ in the Garden of Gethsemane? He prayed drops of blood. [*And being in anguish, he prayed more earnestly, and his sweat was like drops of blood falling to the ground.* Luke 22:44]

[*"*No*" is an answer; and so is "*Wait*"]

January 22

**Philippians 4:13 (KJV)** *I can do all things through Christ which strengtheneth me.*

This verse has always been a favorite verse of mine. It serves as a beacon for me to follow when things get extremely hard. The strength I receive from these words envelops me in God's arms and give me the peace and power to continue. There have been excruciating times in my life, and these words have echoed* in my heart and soul. I emerge from the valleys stronger and wiser, and secure in God's love.

[*I memorized these words in the King James Version, so that's what I hear God whispering in my times of need.]

January 23

**Psalm 56:3** (NIV) *When I am afraid, I put my trust in You.*

I've loved this favorite verse since I was seven years old. It was a memory verse in Sunday School, and not long after I learned it, I had emergency surgery. I don't remember much about the surgery, except that I was scared, and my parents couldn't go down the hall to the operating room with me. The whole time they were rolling me toward the operating room I was reciting that verse to myself. Looking back, I realize that was the first time I understood the importance of Scripture in my life. It is a lesson I've never forgotten.

January 24

**2 Timothy 2:15** (NIV) *Do your best to present yourself to God as one approved, a worker who does not need to be ashamed and who correctly handles the word of truth.*

This favorite verse is another one that's been a part of my life as long as I can remember. I originally learned it in the KJV, but now think the NIV gives a clearer understanding that I am to always be prepared to speak the truth of God to everyone I meet. Not only by my words, but also by my actions. That is sometimes difficult for me, as I get carried away and go on some tangent that really isn't all that important. God has His hands full with my stubborn self. (I heard the amens of my family!)

January 25

***Psalm 23*** (CSB) [1]*The Lord is my shepherd; I have what I need.* [2]*He lets me lie down in green pastures; he leads me beside quiet waters.* [3]*He renews my life; he leads me along the right paths for his name's sake.* [4]*Even when I go through the darkest valley, I fear no danger, for you are with me; your rod and your staff – they comfort me.* [5]*You prepare a table before me in the presence of my enemies; you anoint my head with oil; my cup overflows.* [6]*Only goodness and faithful love will pursue me all the days of my life, and I will dwell in the house of the Lord as long as I live.*

This favorite passage just soothes my soul and blesses my heart each and every time I read or hear it. The pronouns strike me in this chapter – HE-ME (or MY); YOU-YOUR (referring to God), I-MY (ME). They are One for one and make things so personal. I once wrote these words in the margin of my Bible: **The Lord is MY Shepherd, that is all I want or need.** I'm not sure when I wrote those words, but WOW. One day a few years ago, I attended the graveside service of a Jewish friend. The Rabbi began speaking in Hebrew. I didn't know what he was saying, but his words moved me to tears. Once he finished, he said, "Now I'll recite these words in English for our Gentile friends." It was this passage, and my soul was full.

January 26

**<u>Romans 4:21</u>** (NIV) *[*Abraham] being fully persuaded that God had power to do what he had promised.*

This favorite verse gives me hope and peace. The words remind me to be patient when "waiting on God." He **does** have the power to do **all** that He has promised…and He will! I've learned recently that His timing may not be in my lifetime – and that is okay. God never breaks a promise. God is faithful. God is true. God is love. God is God.

[*My interjection.]

January 27

**<u>Psalm 1:1-2</u>** (NIV) [1]*Blessed is the one who does not walk in step with the wicked or stand in the way that sinners take or sit in the company of mockers,* [2]*but whose delight is in the law of the Lord, and who meditates on his law day and night.*

This favorite passage describes the blessed life of someone who walks in the way of the Lord. The last part of verse 2 just warms my soul as I think of meditating on the things of God. When we walk with God daily, we live as God wants us to live. We become the hands and feet of Jesus. O, how we could truly change the world if we'd do this as God intended. Can I get an amen?

January 28

**Philippians 1:9-11** (NIV) [9]*And this is my prayer: that your love may abound more and more in knowledge and depth of insight,* [10]*so that you may be able to discern what is best and may be pure and blameless for the day of Christ,* [11]*filled with the fruit of righteousness that comes through Jesus Christ—to the glory and praise of God.*

These favorite verses, especially verse 10, give me the hope of wisdom on my daily journey; the hope for growth as I walk closely with God; and the hope that one day anyone who comes in contact with me will know I'm a woman of faith just by my actions. I'm not there, yet. I'm a work in progress. God's not finished with me. I'm still growing. I'm still learning.

January 29

**Psalm 30** (MSG) [1]*I give you all the credit, God— you got me out of that mess,you didn't let my foes gloat.* [2]*God, my God, I yelled for help and you put me together.* [3]*God, you pulled me out of the grave, gave me another chance at life when I was down-and-out.* [4]*All you saints! Sing your hearts out to God! Thank him to his face!* [5]*He gets angry once in a while, but across a lifetime there is only love. The nights of crying your eyes out give way to days of laughter.* [6]*When things were going great I crowed, "I've got it made.* [7]*I'm God's favorite. He made me king of the mountain." Then you looked the other way and I fell to pieces.* [8]*I called out to you, God; I laid my case before you:* [9]*Can you sell me for a profit when I'm dead? auction me off at a cemetery yard sale?When I'm 'dust to dust' my songs and stories of you won't sell.* [10]*So, listen! and be kind! Help me out of this!"* [11]*You did it: you changed wild lament into whirling dance; You ripped off my black mourning band and decked me with wildflowers.* [12]*I'm about to burst with song; I can't keep quiet about you. God, my God, I can't thank you enough.*

This passage became a favorite one day in early 2010, when I was enmeshed in one of many family tragedies that have occurred over the years. A friend literally ran into the room to share this Scripture with me. She uses The Message version of the Bible, and the words she read spoke to me in a profound way. My soul sighed a deep breath and I felt whole again as the words came alive healed my soul. Especially verse 11 – "*You did it: you changed wild lament into whirling dance; You ripped off my black mourning band and decked me with wildflowers.*" When life has a choke hold on you, remember this passage. I promise it will help.

January 30

**Proverbs 3:5** (NIV) *Trust in the Lord with all your heart and lean not on your own understanding.*

I learned this favorite verse as a young child. Trusting God allows me to be “okay”, even without understanding everything. Otherwise, I’d be a complete wreck trying to figure out the “why’s” in life. As it is, I rest in His arms and the why’s don’t matter. The WHO is all that matters, and my WHO is God. Peace envelops me, and love infuses me. That’s all I need.

January 31

<u>**John 15: 4-5; 8**</u> (NIV) [4]*Remain in me, as I also remain in you. No branch can bear fruit by itself; it must remain in the vine. Neither can you bear fruit unless you remain in me.* [5]*"I am the vine; you are the branches. If you remain in me and I in you, you will bear much fruit; apart from me you can do nothing.* [8]*This is to my Father's glory, that you bear much fruit, showing yourselves to be my disciples."*

What an incredible analogy Christ spoke to us in this favorite passage! As long as we stay tapped into Him (the Vine), we (the branches) will live. But, if we choose to go our own way, we die. All of us know what branches that have fallen off a tree or other plant look like – withered, brittle, DEAD! That doesn't appeal to me. I'll choose to stay connected to my Vine. Despite my inadequacies, my Vine will nourish and make my wilting branches perk right up in His love. Can I get a witness?

February 1

**Genesis 28:15** (NIV) *I am with you and will watch over you wherever you go, and I will bring you back to this land. I will not leave you until I have done what I have promised you.*

The morning and all its beauty paints an awesome picture of God's love for us. We put our trust in Him, and He walks with us every step of the way. Just as He promised Jacob He wouldn't leave him, He won't leave us. No matter how badly we mess things up, this favorite verse reminds us: HE IS THERE TO DUST US OFF. I have experienced the "dusting off" by God and it is one amazing encounter. He promised to be with me ALWAYS, and He is! When I mess up, He gently picks me up, dusts me off, and helps me deal with the consequences my actions may generate. For a long time, I thought "dusting off" meant erasing; it really means helping me face whatever the future holds, and being with me every step of the way, even as I navigate my consequences.

February 2

**Psalm 46** (CSB) [1]*God is our refuge and strength, a helper who is always found in times of trouble.* [2]*Therefore we will not be afraid, though the earth trembles and the mountains topple into the depths of the seas,* [3]*though its waters roar and foams and the mountains quake with its turmoil.* [4]*There is a river – its streams delight the city of God the holy dwelling place of the Most High.* [5]*God is within her; she will not be toppled. God will help her when the morning dawns.* [6]*Nations rage, kingdoms topple; the earth melts when he lifts his voice.* [7]*The Lord of Armies is with us; the God of Jacob is our stronghold.* [8]*Come, see the works of the Lord, who brings devastation on the earth.* [9] *He makes wars cease throughout the earth. He shatters bows and cuts spears to pieces; he sets wagons ablaze.* [10]*"Stop your fighting, and know that I am God, exalted among the nations, exalted on the earth."* [11]*The Lord of Armies is with us; the God of Jacob is our stronghold.*

This entire chapter is one of my favorites. I first entered this passage into my journal in 2009 after a book signing that didn't go well at all. There were only nine attendees, and six of those were family members! I was extremely disappointed. Psalm 46 spoke to me, helping me to be open to what God had planned, even when everything I'd planned seemed to be going wrong. Listening requires me to STOP! In other translations the words "be still" appear in verse 10 instead of "stop your fighting". How can we be still if we don't stop? We should be in awe of God. The "stopping/being still" part is hard for me, as I'm always in a rush doing one thing or another. I just need to learn to be, just be. May you who also just need to be, just be. Can I get an amen?

February 3

**2 Corinthians 4:13** (NIV*) It is written: "I believed; therefore I have spoken." Since we have that same spirit of faith, we also believe and therefore speak.*

Another favorite verse and one of my mantras. This one explains why I enjoy speaking. The opportunity to share my faith journey with others means a lot to me. I speak because I HAVE heard, and I DO BELIEVE the Gospel. As I have the opportunity, it is not only something I want to do, but something God has led me to do. Am I an expert? Absolutely NOT! But I have experienced God's grace, love, mercy, salvation, peace and many other gifts during my walk with Him. Sharing what He's done for me, not only introduces others to Him, but also reminds me over and over how good God is.

February 4

**Psalm 26:2** (NIV) *Test me, Lord, and try me, examine my heart and my mind.*

King David is crying out to God that he has led a good life, striving to be who God wants him to be. This verse is a favorite, because I can really relate. While I'm far from perfect, I do embrace the teachings of the Scripture and I try to live within God's will. After reading the comments in How to Pray (The Best of John Wesley on Prayer) I think this Psalm was written after King David's affair with Bathsheba. Not only do we know God forgave King David, as He forgives us, we also know King David lived with the consequences of his choices. We also live with our consequences, but as King David cried out to God in this Psalm, we can also cry out and ask Him to help us in our journey of faith.

February 5

**Philippians 4:6** (NIV) *Do not be anxious about anything, but in every situation, by prayer and petition, with thanksgiving, present your requests to God.*

Totally one of my very favorite verses. Have I said that before? Oh, well, it's true. God cares about all our problems – big or small. One day I was running late (actually, that's most days) and Tucker, our hound dog, needed to go out. I let him out and continued running through the house like a hurricane building up speed, throwing on clothes, make-up, doing dishes, and the countless other chores most people do every morning. It was time to leave, so I called him to come in. He didn't come. I called him again, still no sign of Tucker. At this point I got panicky because I was REALLY late and needed him in so I could leave. In desperation, I prayed: "Lord, I know it's silly, but please help me get Tucker inside." At that very moment the skies opened, and rain began pouring!! Tucker scampered inside because he hates rain. A small thing, a trivial thing, but my Heavenly Father, the Maker of all creation stopped to help one of His daughters get her dog inside. And while you may disagree with me on this, and that's okay, nothing is too big; nothing is too small for our God. He knows the number of hairs on our heads. He cares about ALL our concerns. He's there for us always. And He can get a stubborn hound dog in the house! Can I get an amen?

February 6

**Psalm 118:24 (KJV)** *This is the day which the Lord hath made; we will rejoice and be glad in it.*

This is the day the Lord has made, and I am rejoicing! How can this not be a favorite verse? One day I got way behind on e-mails (full disclosure, I STAY behind on emails, and Facebook), so I spent most of the morning reading both and catching up. The good news is I am loved and have many friends! The better news is I can share my faith journey with them! This entry first appeared in my journal on December 8, 2009. Sounds like it was a typical ADHD day in my life! Seriously, though, I love this verse. I learned it from KJV, and to me it is beautiful in that version. The reference to sharing my faith journey is not only a verbal sharing, but also a living witness of the difference He makes in my life. That became even more important to me in 2004, when I became a grandmother for the first time. I pray daily that my grandchildren SEE Christ in me, and I take that responsibility very seriously. Even when Atlanta traffic is a bear! Even when my beloved Atlanta Braves, or my beloved University of Georgia Bulldogs lose. Even when my life is in turmoil – it's still "the day the Lord hath made" and I will rejoice in it; and I will conduct myself accordingly. (I have not perfected the last part of that sentence, but God and I are working on it.)

February 7

**1 Corinthians 13 (KJV)** *[1]Though I speak with the tongues of men and of angels, and have not love, I am become as sounding brass, or a tinkling cymbal. [2]And though I have the gift of prophecy, and understand all mysteries, and all knowledge; and though I have all faith, so that I could remove mountains, and have not love, I am nothing. [3]And though I bestow all my goods to feed the poor, and though I give my body to be burned, and have not love, it profiteth me nothing. [4]Love suffereth long, and is kind; love envieth not; love vaunteth not itself, is not puffed up, [5]Doth not behave itself unseemly, seeketh not her own, is not easily provoked, thinketh no evil; [6]Rejoiceth not in iniquity, but rejoiceth in the truth; [7]Beareth all things, *believeth all things, hopeth all things, endureth all things. [8]Love never faileth: but whether there be prophecies, they shall fail; whether there be tongues, they shall cease; whether there be knowledge, it shall vanish away. [9]For we know in part, and we prophesy in part. [10]But when that which is perfect is come, then that which is in part shall be done away. [11]When I was a child, I spake as a child, I understood as a child, I thought as a child: but when I became a man, I put away childish things.[12] For now we see through a glass, darkly; but then face to face: now I know in part; but then shall I know even as also I am known. [13]And now abideth faith, hope, love, these three; but the greatest of these is love.*

Today is my birthday, so I thought I'd take a walk down memory lane and read a passage I learned years ago when I was 13. I was studying to attain Queen in the Girl's Auxiliary (GA) organization in the Southern Baptist church during the 1960s. This immediately became a favorite passage. I chose to use the King James Version, again because that's the version I used to memorize this chapter, and also because I love the poetry of it.

We were taught to change the word "charity" to "love" throughout, and I've taken the liberty to do that above. The whole passage speaks of how we should live our faith with love. Verse 13 sums it all up so well: *"the greatest of these is love."* From Genesis to Revelation, God's theme is LOVE. God is love. We are His vehicles on this earth to carry and impart His love.

*A note from Pastor Paul: "The Amplified Bible translates this 'Love believes the best in each person.' While not faithful to the Greek in my opinion, it catches the Spirit of Love." Thank you, Pastor Paul, for that insight.*

February 8

**Isaiah 55:6** (NIV) *Seek the Lord while he may be found; call on Him while He is near.*

Sometimes it seems we pack our weekends with one thing after another. I know I do, and the weekend ends up feeling more like a whirlwind. One such weekend occurred in December 2009. There was a ladies' brunch at our church Saturday morning, another meal at our church that evening (Methodists love to eat), the Sunday School Christmas party after the meal, my niece's baptism the following morning, and a family meal at Mom's (Baptist love to eat, too) after the baptism. Whew - makes me tired just writing about it! But in all the hustle and bustle of that weekend, there were life lessons and devotions throughout. One stands out in a profound way to me. When I entered the church for Kaylin's baptism, I couldn't immediately find the family. It occurred to me to just search for Daddy, and sure enough I quickly found him, and once I did, I felt at home. The same is true when we search for our Heavenly Father; once we find Him, we are home. That is why this verse is a favorite.

February 9

**<u>Matthew 22:37-40</u>** (NIV) [37]*Jesus replied: "Love the Lord your God with all your heart and with all your soul and with all your mind.* [38]*This is the first and greatest commandment.* [39]*And the second is like it: Love your neighbor as yourself.* [40]*All the Law and the Prophets hang on these two commandments."*

One of the difficult lessons for me throughout my life has been prioritizing not only my time, but also the things that are important and the things that aren't. This favorite passage nails our faith journey to me. Jesus consolidated the Ten Commandments into two!! As I get older, I find I'm understanding more clearly what's important and what's not. For example, years ago if the UGA (University of Georgia) football team or the Atlanta Braves baseball team lost, I'd go into a funk for days – especially if the games were of dire importance toward a bowl game or a pennant race. I realize now that in the scheme of life winning or losing a sporting event shouldn't be THAT high on our radar. Being the person God created us to be and having a relationship with Him is the defining factor of the balance of our existence. Now, don't get me wrong, I still want my Dawgs and my Braves to win – and I scream pretty loudly (okay, *very* loudly) during the games. However, I don't go into a funk if they lose. Using our hearts – love; souls – communing with God; and minds – THINKING deeply and, as a result, making a difference in this world. Putting God first allows all the other relationships and issues to fall into their proper place.

February 10

**Psalm 62:5-8** (NIV) [5]*Yes, my soul, find rest in God; my hope comes from him.* [6]*Truly he is my rock and my salvation; he is my fortress, I will not be shaken.* [7]*My salvation and my honor depend on God; he is my mighty rock, my refuge.* [8]*Trust in him at all times, you people; pour out your hearts to him, for God is our refuge.*

Life is complicated and just when I think I have something figured out, a curve comes sailing across the home plate of my life. The key is learning how to handle the curves just like professional baseball players learn how to handle real curve balls. This favorite passage spells it out for me. Sometimes it won't equate to a hit, but that's okay – even the greatest players at times strike out! Attitude determines our life's journey and is critically important to people like me, who strike out. I strike out, knowing my hope is in my Coach (the Living God) and that knowledge enables me to keep my chin up and keeps me swinging at the curve balls of life. Occasionally, I get a hit. I do indeed find rest in God.

*As Pastor Paul reviewed this, he noted: "I had the most problem with the change-up". That pitch, too, Pastor Paul – that pitch, too.*

February 11

**Revelation 3:20** (NIV) *Here I am! I stand at the door and knock. If anyone hears my voice and opens the door, I will come in and eat with that person, and they with me.*

One day in November 2009, I decided to make a list of all the things/people I was thankful for.

Family – husband, kids, grandkids, parents, sisters, in-laws, aunts, uncles, cousins – yep, that just about covers it
Friends
Health
Jobs/ability to pay the bills
House
Pets
Food
Opportunities

The list actually goes on and on, as I'm sure it does with each of you. However, most of all I'm thankful for a God Who loved me enough to send His only Son to save me from myself. I love a God Who, if I stop and listen, will speak DIRECTLY to me. It's a no-brainer why this verse of Jesus' words is a favorite.

February 12

**<u>2 Corinthians 13:11</u>** (NIV) *Finally, brothers and sisters, rejoice! Strive for full restoration, encourage one another, be of one mind, live in peace. And the God of love and peace will be with you.*

This journal entry was first written on March 9, 2010.

> **The past several weeks have been a whirlwind, a blur, a nightmare, a time where the events playing out were not the events I would have written had the pen been in my hand. And yet, even with all the "I wish it weren't like this" God has carried us through. I believe it is because for once in my life I stayed focused on Him and just plunged ahead holding His Hand.**
>
> **And even with THAT some of my other plans derailed because as I stayed focused on dealing with the crisis at hand, I sometimes became unfocused on my own goal of healthy eating habits – today I'm back on track.**
>
> **It is amazing how one little "oh that won't hurt" can evolve into a total loss of focus and direction and send you down a path you never intended to explore again. The parallel with our Spiritual life is not falling on deaf ears – it's startling and so real. Praise God He is the Lord of second chances.**

As I include this into *Dancing in God's Love*, it is now 2021, and it's still a favorite verse. I am again finding myself recommitting to the healthy lifestyle I want and need. Over the years I've regained many pounds I thought were gone for good and added several more I'd never met, but apparently wanted to come along on my hips for the ride. I turned to food for comfort rather than staying focused on the God of my Salvation and Peace. Food addiction, like alcohol/ drug/sex/ gambling and all other addictions, is real. I have to embrace the fact that I'm addicted to food, and that I will fight this battle for the rest of my life. However, I'm not alone. I have God, my family, and my friends who walk with me every step of the way. This is a journey, not a destination. I thank God for the second chances I'm continually given in order to get this thing we call life right.

February 13

**<u>Philippians 4:19</u>** (NIV) *And my God will meet all your needs according to the riches of his glory in Christ Jesus.*

This tiny favorite verse is packed with amazing news! The first day of every month it's our responsibility to give the dogs their heart worm pills. They aren't able to do this for themselves. That got me thinking about how God cares for us. Stay with me here – He gives us the:

**pill of salvation**

**pill of righteousness**

**pill of comfort**

**pill of unconditional love**

We just have to hold out our hands and receive the infinite blessings from God each and every day, each and every hour, each and every minute, each and every second.

February 14

**Psalm 73:23-26** (NIV) [23]*Yet I am always with you; you hold me by my right hand.* [24]*You guide me with your counsel, and afterward you will take me into glory.* [25]*Whom have I in heaven but you? And earth has nothing I desire besides you.* [26]*My flesh and my heart may fail, but God is the strength of my heart and my portion forever.*

Sometimes life gets so hectic. I need this favorite passage! Even in our busy and tiring lives, God's Presence covers us – many times by those He sends our way. I'm always in need of resurrection, and I'm so grateful that God places family members and friends in my life that share the burden with me, pray with me, cry with me. In addition to being on the receiving end of those unexpected blessing of the right person being there at the right time, we need to ask God to show us who and how we can help and be *their* right person at the right time. Allowing God to work through us to help another person also blesses us in the process. A win, win, win situation!

February 15

**<u>1 Samuel 16:7</u>** (NIV) *But the Lord said to Samuel, "Do not consider his appearance or his height, for I have rejected him. The Lord does not look at the things people look at. People look at the outward appearance, but the Lord looks at the heart."*

Do the whiskers on my chin change who I am? Of course not. Not any more than a beard on a man changes who he is. Appearances mean a lot to us, but they do NOT change our hearts. They do not change who we are. Only God can change our heart. He can clean off the smut and the dirt. He can sprinkle it with kindness and love. Just as we can change our appearances by plucking the chin hair, God can change our hearts by plucking greed, hatred, envy, lust, etc. from it. So, the next time you're prone to judge someone by their appearance, remember Debi's favorite verse concerning that. I'm telling y'all, it's not easy to not judge, but keeping this verse etched on my heart sure helps me and I hope it will help y'all as well.

February 16

**Psalm 27:1-5** (NIV) [1]*The Lord is my light and my salvation— whom shall I fear? The Lord is the stronghold of my life— of whom shall I be afraid?* [2]*When the wicked advance against me to devour me, it is my enemies and my foes who will stumble and fall.* [3]*Though an army besiege me, my heart will not fear; though war break out against me, even then I will be confident.* [4]*One thing I ask from the Lord, this only do I seek: that I may dwell in the house of the Lord all the days of my life, to gaze on the beauty of the Lord and to seek him in his temple.* [5] *For in the day of trouble he will keep me safe in his dwelling; he will hide me in the shelter of his sacred tent and set me high upon a rock.*

What an incredible Psalm! This favorite passage speaks to me completely and totally where I am. God has a way of speaking through His Word so personally to me, and to each one of you, that it feels like He's just sitting here sharing a cup of coffee and talking with me. Wow, what an awesome and powerful and loving God we have! I remind myself over and over to rest in God's love; rest at His feet; rest in His Word.

February 17

**Matthew 10:13-16** (NIV) [13]*If the home is deserving, let your peace rest on it; if it is not, let your peace return to you.* [14]*If anyone will not welcome you or listen to your words, leave that home or town and shake the dust off your feet.* [15]*Truly I tell you, it will be more bearable for Sodom and Gomorrah on the day of judgment than for that town.* [16]*I am sending you out like sheep among wolves. Therefore, be as shrewd as snakes and as innocent as doves.*

This passage became a favorite quite by accident. As I sat at the table trying to prepare a lesson for Sunday School one morning from the above passage, I was going through all the resources I had and just coming up empty. Nothing was jumping out at me. That's when it struck me that it's a simple story and I was trying to flower it up with impressive knowledge from my learned (pronounced "learn-ed" because it sounds fancy) ways. Too many times we pontificate when all we need to do is tell the simple truth of our Lord. We need to fall on our knees and say *thank you* to our Heavenly Father for all our many blessings. As we carry His story to the world, be ourselves – simple and to the point. Realize everyone doesn't want to hear His story. That is the reason we LIVE THE STORY, and don't just tell the story. Just maybe we'll catch the attention and curiosity of one of them, and they will ask to meet our Lord.

February 18

**<u>Proverbs 20:22</u>** (NIV) *Do not say, "I'll pay you back for this wrong!" Wait for the Lord, and he will avenge you.*

As I reviewed my journals to create this book, a recurring theme was that I allowed the busyness of life to intrude on my time with God. Over and over, I found pages renewing my commitment to spend quality time with God each day – realizing that I need this time as much as I need air, water, and food. I also realized that when I tap into my Power – my Holy Father, my God – I have strength overflowing for the entire day. And then the story of the woman who never ran out of meal for her family came to mind (I Kings 17:7-16), and I understood that my coming to God's table of devotion each day was just like that woman getting meal from the container to prepare her food. I need it to sustain me. I find that when I've spent quality time with God, I'm better equipped to deal with people who treat me badly. This verse is a favorite because in addition to curbing my desire for revenge, I am much healthier, happier, content, and productive because God helps me in all that I do.

February 19

**1 Corinthians 6:19** (NIV) *Do you not know that your bodies are temples of the Holy Spirit, who is in you, whom you have received from God? You are not your own.*

Even though I know the passage this verse comes from is primarily addressing sexual sins, for me it screams at me regarding my food addiction. This is a favorite verse that cuts to the chase. I've read several books and articles designed to help me understand and overcome my love affair with food. I know my over-eating is a sin against my body, just as sexual sins are sins against the body. Gluttony is one of the seven deadly sins, and I have been guilty of it most of my adult life. As I write this, I work daily to stay on my game with healthy living – eating healthy, exercising regularly, getting enough sleep, etc. Keeping the truth that my body IS A TEMPLE foremost in my mind spurs me on the right path.

February 20

<u>**Psalm139:13-14, 23-24**</u> (NIV) [13]*For you created my inmost being; you knit me together in my mother's womb.* [14]*I praise you because I am fearfully and wonderfully made; your works are wonderful, I know that full well.* [23]*Search me, God, and know my heart; test me and know my anxious thoughts.* [24]*See if there is any offensive way in me, and lead me in the way everlasting.*

I love the poetry of the Psalms. "You knit me together in my mother's womb" is a beautiful phrase to me. Both of my grandmothers sewed, and I remember their hands painstakingly following the patterns to make beautiful items. Our God, our Creator, handmade each of us, and so often we let life keep us from communing with Him. Time truly gets away from the well-intentioned and I end up (like most people) not doing the very thing that is important to me. It's a matter of setting priorities. What a great favorite passage to help me with this life challenge. The first thing I should do every morning is acknowledge God and His place in my life. The last thing I should do every night is acknowledge God and His place in my life. Isn't it wonderful and amazing that the very thing felt by me today, was felt by the Psalmist!! (I truly hope that is a real word). I thank God for helping me line up the priorities in my life as I continue my personal journey. I also thank God for loving me even when my priorities are off-kilter.

February 21

**Hebrews 11:1** (NIV) *Now faith is confidence in what we hope for and assurance about what we do not see.*

FAITH is a *huge* five-letter word – but it is this five-letter word that fuels my very existence. Without FAITH I could not put one foot before the other. Without FAITH I would have no hope. Without FAITH I would have no joy. Without FAITH I would have no reason to live. My FAITH is in Jesus Christ, my Creator, My Savior. I don't understand it all any more than I understand electricity or how a huge metal plane (or small one, for that matter) stays in the sky – but it happens. When I flip a switch, I have FAITH the light will come on; and when I fly I have FAITH the plane will stay in the sky. This favorite verse reminds me to acknowledge God's goodness and greatness – being in awe of Who He is. My dear friend, Debra Brumley, once told me that "faith" was a verb. I looked it up, and sure enough, it's a transit verb – albeit archaic according to the dictionary. I'm thinking we need to bring it back as a verb! Like Debra said, "The more you do, the stronger you get." The more you exercise your faith, the stronger it is. Always believing and knowing that no matter the specifics of a situation, God is there. God is Love. God is God.

February 22

**Psalm 146** (CSB) [1]*Hallelujah! My soul, praise the Lord.* [2]*I will praise the Lord all my life; I will sing to my God as long as I live.* [3]*Do not trust in nobles, in a son of man, who cannot save.* [4]*When his breath leaves him, he returns to the ground; on that day his plans die.* [5]*Happy is the one whose help is the God of Jacob, whose hope is in the Lord his God,* [6]*the Maker of heaven and earth, the sea and everything in them. He remains faithful forever,* [7]*executing justice for the exploited and giving food to the hungry. The Lord frees prisoners.* [8]*The Lord opens the eyes of the blind. The Lord raises up those who are oppressed. The Lord loves the righteous.* [9]*The Lord protects resident aliens and helps the fatherless and the widow, but he frustrates the ways of the wicked.* [10]*The Lord reigns forever, Zion, your God reigns for all generations. Hallelujah!*

Most of the time I'm asleep within five minutes of my head hitting the pillow. However, occasionally I'm not able to sleep for one reason or another. On April 5, 2010, it occurred to me as I lay tossing and turning, to get up and spend time with God. Not coincidentally, the Scripture reading in the devotion book I was using was Psalm 146. It became a favorite passage on the spot! Since that night, there have been many times that I've gotten up and spent time with God instead of tossing and turning. Each and every time I've been able to go right to sleep once I was back in bed. Sometimes I read Scripture, sometimes I pray – the point is I spend time with Him. This is all the evidence I need to be convinced that my being connected and tapped into my Source is essential in my life. My Source is Holy God.

February 23

**<u>Luke 2:25-32</u>** *(CSB)* [25]*There was a man in Jerusalem whose name was Simeon. This man was righteous and devout, looking forward to Israel's consolation, and the Holy Spirit was on him.* [26]*It had been revealed to him by the Holy Spirit that he would not see death before he saw the Lord's Messiah.* [27]*Guided by the Spirit, he entered the temple. When the parents brought in the child Jesus to perform for him what was customary under the law,* [28]*Simeon took him up in his arms, praised God, and said,* [29]*"Now, Master, you can now dismiss your servant in peace, as you promised.* [30]*For my eyes have seen your salvation.* [31]*You have prepared it in the sight of all peoples –* [32]*a light for revelation to the Gentile, and glory toyour people Israel."*

Simeon held onto a dream that he would see the Messiah. How often do we have dreams and let them go when things get tough? What makes us different than Simeon? I believe the difference was his faith. His faith was so strong. He is defined in the Bible as righteous and devout – meaning he was good, and he was embedded in the studies of Scripture. To embed a file or object is to take it and put it into another file so it becomes part of the new file. When we embed Christ into our hearts, we become the Christians of Faith we are meant to be. We become in-tune with God – knowing His will for us, and living it out. This is a favorite passage because it reminds me to stay focused on Christ.

February 24

**<u>Genesis 5:21-24</u>** (NIV) [21]*When Enoch had lived 65 years, he became the father of Methuselah.* [22]*After he became the father of Methuselah, Enoch walked faithfully with God 300 years and had other sons and daughters.* [23]*Altogether, Enoch lived a total of 365 years.* [24]*Enoch walked faithfully with God; then he was no more, because God took him away.*

Walk with God!! So simple and yet we make it so hard. A favorite passage because it tells about Enoch. Enoch was a man who walked with God – that was his testimony. Oh, that "she walked with God" would be my testimony. Walking with God to me is fresh air, blue sky, temperature in the high 60's, soft wind blowing, and the sounds of nature playing the song that only Nature can play! And the neat thing is, when we walk with God, we experience what I've just described even on the most horrible of days. Can I get a witness?!

February 25

**John 1:14** (NIV) *The Word became flesh and made his dwelling among us. We have seen his glory, the glory of the one and only Son, who came from the Father, full of grace and truth.*

Oh my, this favorite verse touches my soul deeply each and every time I read or hear it. “Dear Lord, the power within me comes from You and You alone. Power to get through the day, power to function, power to love, power to forgive, power to accomplish the tasks I have. Thank You for being IN me. Thank You for caring enough to come to this earth and teach me – living as I live, feeling as I feel. Amen and Amen.”

February 26

**<u>Psalm 127:1</u>** (NIV) *Unless the Lord builds the house, the builders labor in vain. Unless the Lord watches over the city, the guards stand watch in vain.*

WOW – one phone call and life as we know it changes. This entry in 2010 was a few days after finding out yet more devastating news in our family. We circled the wagons and hunkered down (that's a Georgia phrase meaning we supported one another - try to stay with me here). The myriad of thoughts racing through my mind felt like a movie trailer – and yet it wasn't; it was real life, and MINE at that! It was hard to breathe, hard to fathom the pain. I wasn't in any starring role of this particular "life movie", so all I could do was sit back and watch it unfold before my eyes. Searching the Scriptures, I found Psalm 127 which, you guessed it, became a favorite. God always leads me to just the passage I need when I truly search. "It is well with my soul". The world may be falling apart at my feet, but God sees me through and is there for me. It **is** Well with my soul.

February 27

**Romans 12:4-8** (NIV) [4]*For just as each of us has one body with many members, and these members do not all have the same function,* [5]*so in Christ we, though many, form one body, and each member belongs to all the others.* [6]*We have different gifts according to the grace given to each of us. If your gift is prophesying, then prophesy in accordance with your faith;* [7]*if it is serving, then serve; if it is teaching, then teach;* [8]*if it is to encourage, then give encouragement; if it is giving, then give generously; if it is to lead, do it diligently; if it is to show mercy, do it cheerfully.*

All of us have different strengths and weaknesses. We also have different talents. I play the piano, but I'm NOT an accomplished pianist because it isn't one of my strengths. It's just something I enjoy doing for my own pleasure. Praying for guidance and knowing our strengths, and developing those strengths, will help us all as we strive to do God's work. Being what and who He needs us to be should be foremost in our lives. This favorite passage reminds me to be and do what God uniquely created me to be and do.

February 28

**Psalm 29:2, 11** (NIV) [2]*Ascribe to the Lord the glory due his name; worship the Lord in the splendor of his holiness.* [11]*The Lord gives strength to his people; the Lord blesses his people with peace.*

***Another* phone call – another family situation; another opportunity for God to pour out His love on me.** I was mentally, emotionally and physically tired that morning in 2010 when I initially entered these words into my journal. I'd spent the weekend with my best friend, Iris, who was beginning the last stages of her battle with early-onset Alzheimer's. I went to work knowing all my pistons weren't firing, but knowing also God would make up the difference…and He did. Then my cell rings and it's my dad telling me Mom was not feeling well and my older sister, Kathy, had taken her to the ER. I told him I'd be there as soon as I could. The relief in his voice was so unmistakable it brought tears to my eyes. I quickly tied loose ends at the office, hurried home, packed and headed to my parents' house. It seemed our family was in one of those "what next?" phases, and I realized my new motto was "bring it on, Satan; God's on my side." As it turned out, Mom was having a panic attack, and was fine. And I spent a wonderful evening with my parents – which was a special and rare treat. These favorite verses are a special and rare treat as well. Can I get an amen?

February 29

**Psalm 37** (CSB) [1]*Do not be agitated by evildoers; do not envy those who do wrong.* [2]*For they whither quickly like grass and wilt like tender green plants.* [3]*Trust in the Lord and do what is good; dwell in the land and live securely.* [4]*Take delight in the Lord, and he will give you your heart's desires.* [5]*Commit your way to the Lord; trust in him and he will act,* [6]*making your righteousness shine like the dawn, your justice like the noonday.* [7]*Be silent before the Lord and wait expectantly for him; do not be agitated by one who prospers in his way, by the person who carries out evil plans.* [8]*Refrain from anger and give up your rage; do not be agitated—it can only bring harm.* [9]*For evildoers will be destroyed, but those who put their hope in the Lord will inherit the land.* [10]*A little while, and the wicked person will be no more; though you look for him, he will not be there.* [11]*But the humble will inherit the land and will enjoy abundant prosperity.* [12]*The wicked person schemes against the righteous and gnashes his teeth at him.* [13]*The Lord laughs at him because he sees that his day is coming.* [14]*The wicked have drawn the sword and strung the bow to bring down the poor and needy and to slaughter those whose way is upright.* [15]*Their swords will enter their own hearts, and their bows will be broken.* [16]*The little that the righteous person has is better than the abundance of many wicked people.* [17]*For the arms of the wicked will be broken, but the Lord supports the righteous.* [18]*The Lord watches over the blameless all their days, and their inheritance will last forever.* [19]*They will not be disgraced in times of adversity; they will be satisfied in days of hunger.* [20]*But the wicked will perish; the Lord's enemies like the glory of the pastures will fade away – they will fade like smoke.* [21]*The wicked person borrows and does not repay, but the righteous one is gracious and giving.* [22]*Those who are blessed by the Lord will inherit the land, but those cursed by him will be destroyed.* [23]*A person's steps are established by the Lord, and he takes pleasure in his way.* [24]*Though he falls, he will not be overwhelmed because the Lord supports him with his hand.* [25]*I* *have been young and now I am old, yet I have not seen the righteous abandoned or his children begging for bread. [26]He is always generous, always lending, and his children are a blessing. [27]Turn away from evil, do what is good, and settle permanently. [28]For the Lord loves justice and will not abandon his faithful ones. They are kept safe forever, but the children of the wicked will be destroyed. [29]The righteous will inherit the land and dwell in it permanently. [30]The mouth of the righteous utters wisdom;, his tongue speaks what is just. [31]The instruction of his God is in his heart; his steps do not falter. [32]The wicked one lies in wait for the righteous and intends to kill him; [33]the Lord will not leave him in the power of the wicked one or allow him to be condemned when he is judged. [34]Wait for the Lord and keep his way, and he will exalt you to inherit the land. You will watch when the wicked are destroyed. [35]I have seen a wicked, violent person well-rooted, like a flourishing native tree. [36]Then I passed by and noticed he was gone; I searched for him, but he could not be found. [37]Watch the blameless and observe the upright, for the person of peace will have a future. [38]But transgressors will all be eliminated; the future of the wicked will be destroyed. [39]The salvation of the righteous is from the Lord, their refuge in a time of distress. [40]The Lord helps and delivers them; he will deliver them from the wicked and will save them because they take refuge in him.*

So much for a short and quick devotion… Seriously, though, I couldn't pick a favorite verse from Chapter 37. The entire passage just speaks volumes (no pun intended) to me. When I feel my world imploding, I hold onto the Truth that I am God's, and He will **always hold me.** Y'all are God's too, and He'll hold all y'all, too.

I realize today's entry is much longer than most, but it's the 29th of February. Even if you use this book every year, you only read this one once every four years…just sayin'. ☺

March 1

**<u>Psalm 34:4, 8, 18</u>** (NIV) [4]*I sought the Lord, and he answered me; he delivered me from all my fears.* [8]*Taste and see that the Lord is good; blessed is the one who takes refuge in him.* [18]*The Lord is close to the brokenhearted and saves those who are crushed in spirit.*

The entire chapter is filled with comfort. I love reading those verses because I just feel bathed in God's mercy and in His love. These three favorite verses jumped out at me as if they were written just for me! I have lived those verses many times. I am so thankful for a God who hears and cares. A God Whose very Word comforts and soothes my soul.

March 2

**<u>Romans 3:23-25</u>** (NIV) [23]*for all have sinned and fall short of the glory of God,* [24]*and all are justified freely by his grace through the redemption that came by Christ Jesus.* [25]*God presented Christ as a sacrifice of atonement, through the shedding of his blood—to be received by faith. He did this to demonstrate his righteousness, because in his forbearance he had left the sins committed beforehand unpunished—*

Over and over, I run out of the house to do this or that, or I jump right into a project at the house without meaning to "forget" God, and yet I do. When this happens, I have in essence left Him totally out of the equation of my daily life. Absolutely not my intention, but in reality, it happens more often than it should. Praise God for His AMAZING GRACE that bathes me in His love in spite of myself. He provides me with favorite verses that speak to my soul.

March 3

**Proverbs 19:21** (NIV) *Many are the plans in a person's heart, but it is the Lord's purpose that prevails.*

Have you ever inadvertently hurt someone? I have. One day several years ago, I had several things on my platter, and one was to meet my daughter, Jeri, at the mall for an afternoon of mother-daughter shopping. During the course of the day, she contacted me and said she'd rather just stay home instead of go shopping. So, instead of heading to her house, I headed home to get some chores done – only to realize much later she was expecting me at her house to just visit with each other! I felt terrible that I'd disappointed her. This passage in Proverbs reminded me that I needed to align myself with God's purpose in my life. While I would NEVER intentionally hurt anyone, I realized that day the importance of being in tune with the needs of others in order to know when someone is reaching out to me. Have y'all noticed that my favorite verses are the ones that speak to me and keep me on track? I'm telling you, God has His hands full with me!

March 4

**<u>Luke 17:11-19</u>** (CSB) *[11]While traveling to Jerusalem, he [*Jesus] passed between Samaria and Galilee. [12]As he entered a village, ten men with leprosy met him. They stood at a distance [13]and raised their voices saying, "Jesus, Master, have mercy on us!" [14]When he saw them, he told them, "Go and show yourselves to the priests." And while they were going, they were cleansed. [15]But one of them, seeing that he was healed, returned and, with a loud voice, gave glory to God. [16]He fell face down at his feet, thanking him. And he was a Samaritan. [17]Then Jesus said, "Were not ten cleansed? Where are the nine? [18]Didn't any return to give glory to God except this foreigner?" [19]And he told him, "Get up and go on your way. Your faith has saved you."*

This favorite passage speaks to me in two ways. One – it reminds me to be thankful for what I have, and to pray thanksgiving prayers. So many times we approach God with our wants and desires, and once we have what we asked Him for we neglect to say thank you. Two – it reminds me that people who are different from me, who are "foreign" to my way of thinking, are still God's children and are not necessarily wrong just because they disagree with me. Jesus stopped, spoke to them, and healed them. God is NOT a respecter of persons. That means, He loves us all equally – no favorites! This message is not only conveyed in the above passage but is also in other passages throughout the Bible. See 2 Chronicles 19:7, Acts 10:34, Romans 2:11, and Galatians 3:28, just to name a few. It's pretty clear, y'all – no race nor creed has the inside track with God. We're ALL His children. Can I get an amen?

[*My interjection.]

March 5

**<u>Hosea 10:12</u>** (NIV) *Sow righteousness for yourselves, reap the fruit of unfailing love, and break up your unplowed ground; for it is time to seek the Lord, until he comes and showers his righteousness on you.*

God led me to the above Scripture on June 1, 2010. The morning had started out great with my daily exercise routine – and then it seemed everything went downhill from there. I was left with just the minimum amount of time for a quick devotion. I offered up a desperate prayer asking if there was any verse God could lead me to in this brief moment I had to spend with him. And just like that, I was led to Hosea 10:12, a new favorite verse!! It IS time – He is here!

March 6

**<u>Hebrews 12:14-17</u>** (MSG) [14-17]*Work at getting along with each other and with God. Otherwise you'll never get so much as a glimpse of God. Make sure no one gets left out of God's generosity. Keep a sharp eye out for weeds of bitter discontent. A thistle or two gone to seed can ruin a whole garden in no time. Watch out for the Esau syndrome: trading away God's lifelong gift in order to satisfy a short-term appetite. You well know how Esau later regretted that impulsive act and wanted God's blessing —but by then it was too late, tears or no tears.*

The lessons in this favorite passage are simple – put God and His truths first in your life. Get along with and take care of each other. Don't be bitter – not even a little, because it will get out of hand just like weeds and choke out the good. Don't throw away your life/dreams for a brief moment of satisfaction. The words of The Message version speak to me so clearly. Our family has been touched by the pain of addiction, and we've seen firsthand someone throwing their life away for a passing thrill. I, myself, have taken way too many years to reach a healthy weight goal because I choose a brief moment of satisfying my sweet tooth rather than staying on course with healthy choices. After reading this passage, I will think twice about my healthy living versus "satisfying a short-term appetite".

March 7

**Isaiah 60:1** (NIV) *Arise, shine, for your light has come, and the glory of the Lord rises upon you.*

The first time I remember learning this favorite verse was in 1962 when I was nine years old and had just joined GA's (Girl's Auxiliary) in the Southern Baptist Church I attended. This was our watchword. As I write this, I'm 68 years old and I remember this verse, plus the "five star-ideals":

Abiding in Him through prayer
Advancing in wisdom by Bible study
Adorning myself with good works
Acknowledging my stewardship of time, money, and personality
Accepting the challenge of the Great Commission

Two things come to mind: 1) we have God's Light shining on us and we should live our lives accordingly, and 2) the meaningful things we learn as children stay with us. Therefore, teach our children and grandchildren so they, too, will have this comfort in their golden years.

March 8

**2 Peter 1:12** (NIV) *So I will always remind you of these things, even though you know them and are firmly established in the truth you now have.*

Peter is reminding us of what we already know. Having been in church since I was two weeks old, I imagine I've heard most (if not all) of the Scripture. And yet, I sill learn because each and every time I earnestly approach God's Word, He speaks to me through it. I mentioned in the foreword of this book that sometimes the same favorite Scripture will speak differently depending on where we are in our journey on any given day. We need to be open to that, as well as to the fact we need reminders of Whose we are and how we should live. Can I get a witness?

March 9

**Jeremiah 9:23-24** (NIV) [23]This is what the Lord says: *"Let not the wise boast of their wisdom or the strong boast of their strength or the rich boast of their riches, [24]but let the one who boasts boast about this: that they have the understanding to know me, that I am the Lord, who exercises kindness, justice and righteousness on earth, for in these I delight," declares the Lord.*

This passage is a favorite because it really tells it like it **should** be. It contains powerful words that encapsulate our relationship as it should be with God. The only thing we truly have to boast about is God. We tend to feel right proud of the things we've accumulated in our lives, or of the things we've accomplished. My prayer is that the next time I'm tempted to toot my own horn, or even feel proud of myself, I remember Whose I am, stop, and give thanks.

March 10

**2 Corinthians 9:7** (NIV) *Each of you should give what you have decided in your heart to give, not reluctantly or under compulsion, for God loves a cheerful giver.*

This favorite verse speaks of being a cheerful giver. God wants us to give because we truly WANT to give, not because we feel compelled to give. So many of us in the USA have enough to spare, and we should cheerfully give of what we have. I've heard it said that you can tell about someone's heart by what's in the checkbook. That statement had a profound effect upon me! When God asks me "what's in YOUR wallet?", I don't want to be ashamed or embarrassed. I want to know I've heeded His Word and given as He would – cheerfully and completely.

March 11

**<u>Nehemiah 1:1-4</u>** (MSG) [1-2]*The memoirs of Nehemiah, son of Hacaliah. It was the month of Kislev in the twentieth year. At the time I was in the palace complex at Susa. Hanani, one of my brothers, had just arrived from Judah with some fellow Jews. I asked them about the conditions among the Jews there who had survived the exile, and about Jerusalem.* [3]*They told me, "The exile survivors who are left there in the province are in bad shape. Conditions are appalling. The wall of Jerusalem is still rubble; the city gates are still cinders."* [4]*When I heard this, I sat down and wept. I mourned for days, fasting and praying before the God-of-Heaven.*

**<u>Nehemiah 2:4-5</u>** (MSG) [4-5]*The king then asked me, "So what do you want?" Praying under my breath to the God-of-Heaven, I said, "If it please the king, and if the king thinks well of me, send me to Judah, to the city where my family is buried, so that I can rebuild it."*

Nehemiah felt the need to rebuild Jerusalem, and he put a plan of action together to do so. As I read these favorite verses, I felt a need to be instrumental in God's love becoming vital in America. The overhead light above my table where I was reading this passage brightened for the first time in quite a while. A sign from God? Perhaps. Regardless, when I see the hate and disharmony of our great country, I hear God telling me to **do something.** It reminds me of the gospel song *Do Something* by Matthew West. The lyrics indicate the man sees all the bad in the world and says to God, "why don't You do something?" – and God replies, "I did. I created you." God has created us to **do something**, so let's do it. Amen?

March 12

**<u>John 1:41</u>** (NIV) *The first thing Andrew did was to find his brother Simon and tell him, "We have found the Messiah" (that is, the Christ).*

How wonderful is it that Andrew's first action after meeting Jesus was to go tell his brother?! There isn't a lot to elaborate on this other than to remind myself and anyone reading this that we should "go and do likewise". This favorite verse is truly a no-brainer, as the kids say. Sharing our faith, and what God has done for us, is the greatest legacy we can leave our family, friends, and our world.

March 13

**<u>Psalm 61:2-3</u>** (NIV) [2]*From the ends of the earth I call to you, I call to you as my heart grows faint; lead me to the rock that is higher than I.* [3]*For you have been my refuge, a strong tower against the foe.*

I suspect that this Psalm, like so many, was written while David was fleeing for his life. The NLT uses the words “is overwhelmed” in verse 2 rather than “grows faint” which may resonate better in our day and time than “grows faint”. We are bombarded with pressures from everywhere. What a blessing to know and feel God’s LOVE and STRENGTH in those times! And how cool is it that His divinely inspired Word has verses like these to become our favorites – because they touch our very soul.

March 14

**1 Corinthians 10:13** (MSG) *No test or temptation that comes your way is beyond the course of what others have had to face. All you need to remember is that God will never let you down; he'll never let you be pushed past your limit; he'll always be there to help you come through it.*

God was surely sending Scripture to us the week that we thought the trial for the fourth and final defendant accused of murdering our sister would begin. Sometimes God guides us to a verse, and other times he uses a friend to share a verse with you. My dear friend, Kristi Gass, shared this one with me that week. What a comfort this favorite verse is to know God will NEVER let us down.

March 15

**<u>Psalm 100</u>** (MSG) [1-2]*On your feet now—applaud God! Bring a gift of laughter, sing yourselves into his presence.* [3]*Know this: God is God, and God, God. He made us; we didn't make him. We're his people, his well-tended sheep.* [4]*Enter with the password: "Thank you!" Make yourselves at home, talking praise. Thank him. Worship him.* [5]*For God is sheer beauty, all-generous in love, loyal always and ever.*

There's really not a whole lot I can add to this favorite Psalm. It is usually read around Thanksgiving but should be read over and over throughout the year, throughout our lives. I normally prefer the King James Version since that is how I memorized it. However, this version touched my soul, too, and I felt it may touch y'all's also. Praise God from Whom ALL blessings flow!! Doesn't it just fill your heart? Doesn't it give a boost to your day? Can I get an amen, y'all?

March 16

**Romans 14;10-19** (NLT) *[10]So why do you condemn another believer? Why do you look down on another believer? Remember, we will all stand before the judgment seat of God. [11]For the Scriptures say, "'As surely as I live,' says the Lord, 'every knee will bend to me, and every tongue will declare allegiance to God'." [12]Yes, each of us will give a personal account to God. [13]So let's stop condemning each other. Decide instead to live in such a way that you will not cause another believer to stumble and fall. [14]I know and am convinced on the authority of the Lord Jesus that no food, in and of itself, is wrong to eat. But if someone believes it is wrong, then for that person it is wrong. [15]And if another believer is distressed by what you eat, you are not acting in love if you eat it. Don't let your eating ruin someone for whom Christ died. [16]Then you will not be criticized for doing something you believe is good. [17]For the Kingdom of God is not a matter of what we eat or drink, but of living a life of goodness and peace and joy in the Holy Spirit. [18]If you serve Christ with this attitude, you will please God, and others will approve of you, too. [19]So then, let us aim for harmony in the church and try to build each other up.*

These verses are favorites because they burn a fire in my soul. No matter who we are or where we are, people will disagree with our choices. The goal is to respectfully be true to ourselves and our beliefs, and with God's help be nonjudgmental and respectful of others. It has been my experience that Christians fall short on this. I heard it said once that the Christian Army was the only army that killed its wounded, and I've seen that happen. My intent in repeating this is not to offend, but to be a wake-up call to the Christian community. Jesus said, *"By this everyone will know that you are my disciples, if you love one another."* (John 13:35 NIV). I'm pretty sure that's still true…just sayin'.

March 17th

**<u>Ecclesiastes 3:1-8</u>** (CSB)_

1 *There is an occasion for everything,*
*and a time for every activity under heaven:*
2 *a time to give birth and a time to die;*
*a time to plant and a time to uproot;*
3 *a time to kill and a time to heal;*
*a time to tear downand a time to build;*
4 *a time to weep and a time to laugh;*
*a time to mourn and a time to dance;*
5 *a time to throw stones and a time to gather stones;*
*a time to embrace and a time to avoid embracing;*
6 *a time to search and a time to count as lost;*
*a time to keep and a time to throw away;*
7 *a time to tear and a time to sew;*
*a time to be silent and a time to speak;*
8 *a time to love and a time to hate;*
*a time for war and a time for peace.*

Solomon's words are beautiful and became a favorite passage to me when I was in my teens. He recognized and articulated what's been true since the beginning – a time for everything. The cycles of life have not changed. Each and every one of us experience life as described in this passage. It is a comfort to know that God is still in control. As we honor and worship Him, we find the cycles of our lives more manageable and we find ourselves more at peace.

[Author's note: Full disclosure… I learned this passage from the rock song, *Turn! Turn! Turn!* released by The Byrds in 1965. Goes to show God's Word can be found everywhere.]

March 18

**<u>2 Thessalonians 3:5</u>** (NLT) *May the Lord lead your hearts into a full understanding and expression of the love of God and the patient endurance that comes from Christ.*

The journal date of this favorite verse was February 17, 2015. At the time, we were expecting the fourth and final defendant in the murder of our sister, Gail, to go to trial the following week. Jo Ellen, my youngest sister, had begun posting verses on Facebook. This one reached out and grabbed my heart and became a favorite that day. God uses people. God uses social media. God uses events. God uses anything that touches another person to get His Message across. He loves us. He's patient with us. He endures and helps us endure. Amen and amen.

March 19

**Psalm 55:22** (NIV) *Cast your cares on the Lord and he will sustain you; he will never let the righteous be shaken.*

Favorite verses like this one surely explain how I get through this journey we call life. Without the Power of God to hold me up and care for me through ALL that happens, I do NOT know how I would get along. I put one foot in front of the other because my God is there to guide me and love me. There are times I know He carries me, because I'm not capable to go on without Him. Let this verse touch your soul.

March 20

**Romans 12:1** (NIV) *Therefore, I urge you, brothers and sisters, in view of God's mercy, to offer your bodies as a living sacrifice, holy and pleasing to God—this is your true and proper worship.*

This verse is a favorite because it "keeps me real". It reminds me that my total self – everything about me – mind, heart, soul – is to be committed to God. Paul is urging us to live our best life, reading, studying, and poring over all the things of God's Word.

[Author's note: As I originally typed this, I made a typo that ended the second sentence with the word *Go* rather than *God.* A slip-up on my part for sure; but a revealing message from God to GO and speak/write of Him.]

March 21

**Psalm 63:1-2** (NIV) [1]*You, God, are my God, earnestly I seek you; I thirst for you, my whole being longs for you, in a dry and parched land where there is no water.* [2]*I have seen you in the sanctuary and beheld your power and your glory.*

These verses are favorites because they touch my soul. Keeping in touch with God allows us to live by faith, and then see and experience His power and glory in our lives. No explanations, just faith in our God. I originally wrote those sentences in December 2010. You might say that apparently, I'd never had a real problem, but our family had faced many challenges that year - difficult, heart wrenching challenges, and our faith (no answers to our questions), just our faith got us through. Since then, within a six-month period, our family faced the murder of my sister, Daddy's death from Alzheimer's, and the death of my 3-year-old great-nephew. We're still standing, and it's because of our faith in God – nothing more.

March 22

**I Corinthians 2:6-16** (NLT) [6]*Yet when I am among mature believers, I do speak with words of wisdom, but not the kind of wisdom that belongs to this world or to the rulers of this world, who are soon forgotten.* [7]*No, the wisdom we speak of is the mystery of God—his plan that was previously hidden, even though he made it for our ultimate glory before the world began.* [8]*But the rulers of this world have not understood it; if they had, they would not have crucified our glorious Lord.* [9]*That is what the Scriptures mean when they say, "No eye has seen, no ear has heard, and no mind has imagined what God has prepared for those who love him."* [10]*But it was to us that God revealed these things by his Spirit. For his Spirit searches out everything and shows us God's deep secrets.* [11]*No one can know a person's thoughts except that person's own spirit, and no one can know God's thoughts except God's own Spirit.* [12]*And we have received God's Spirit (not the world's spirit), so we can know the wonderful things God has freely given us.* [13]*When we tell you these things, we do not use words that come from human wisdom. Instead, we speak words given to us by the Spirit, using the Spirit's words to explain spiritual truths.* [14]*But people who aren't spiritual can't receive these truths from God's Spirit. It all sounds foolish to them and they can't understand it, for only those who are spiritual can understand what the Spirit means.* [15]*Those who are spiritual can evaluate all things, but they themselves cannot be evaluated by others.* [16]*For, "Who can know the Lord's thoughts? Who knows enough to teach him?" But we understand these things, for we have the mind of Christ.*

Verse 9 always jumps out at me because I recognize that no human words could possibly capture the incredible plans God has for us. And while I know I'll never completely understand the mind or ways of God, verse 16 assures me that I'll better understand what's in store for me through Christ. Staying in tune with Him through prayer and Bible study helps clear the fog. Even for this ADHD writer, this favorite passage assures me the fog will clear.

[Author’s note: The quote in verse 9 is from Isaiah 64:4; the quote in verse 16 is Isaiah 40:13].

March 23

**Psalm 91:4, 11** (NIV) [4]*He will cover you with his feathers, and under his wings you will find refuge; his faithfulness will be your shield and rampart.* [11]*For he will command his angels concerning you to guard you in all your ways.*

What powerful verses these two are! They immediately became favorites as I imagined God pulling us under His wings like a mama bird. They state without question the protection we have in God. Isn't it comforting to know the angels are watching over and guarding us? Service men and women use Chapter 91 to comfort them in battle. The picture in my mind's eye is one of peace, love, and safety. I encourage y'all to read the entire chapter.

March 24

**<u>I Thessalonians 5:16-18</u>** (NIV) [16]*Rejoice always,* [17]*pray continually,* [18]*give thanks in all circumstances; for this is God's will for you in Christ Jesus.*

Verse 18 really bothered me until a preacher pointed out it reads IN not FOR all circumstances. That insight makes it easier for me to grasp the meaning of the verse, and once I did, this passage became a favorite. My family has weathered many tragedies since January 2010. The kind you read about in the papers, see on the news and occasionally in movies but never imagine it could happen to you or one of yours. And through it all, God has walked with us and/or carried us. And for HIM we give thanks. For HIM Who is there when we can't put one foot in front of the other. For HIM Who, when we don't know what/how to pray, makes intercession for us.

March 25

**<u>Psalm 127:1-5</u>** (MSG) [1-2]*If God doesn't build the house, the builders only build shacks. If God doesn't guard the city, the night watchman might as well nap. It's useless to rise early and go to bed late, and work your worried fingers to the bone. Don't you know he enjoys giving rest to those he loves?* [3-5]*Don't you see that children are God's best gift? the fruit of the womb his generous legacy? Like a warrior's fistful of arrows are the children of a vigorous youth. Oh, how blessed are you parents, with your quivers full of children! Your enemies don't stand a chance against you; you'll sweep them right off your doorstep.*

As I was deciding which favorite Scriptures to use, I ran across an entry dated March 14, 2011. The only verses from this passage entered that day were verses 3-5. But today God laid on my heart to include verses 1-2 as well. I stated earlier that when we're open to God, Scripture might mean different things to us on different days depending on where we are in our journey. He KNOWS us so well, and He brings His message to us! Recently I have found myself staying up late writing this book, only to realize how tired I am – to the point of nodding off as I *type! Now that is totally ridiculous, right? God's message to me right here, right now: "go to bed when you're tired. Get a good night's sleep. The writing will be right here for you in the morning." The message to me from verses 3-5 is that for those of us with children to realize they are gifts we have, and we are to use our time with them wisely. These verses in NO way knock those who are childless or, in anyway mean they are not blessed of God. One of the most important "mothers" in my life was my first boss, Roslyn LaTorre. She's gone to be with our Lord now, but her "quivers were full of children," even though she didn't give birth to any of us. She was a role model to her nieces, nephews, and those of us fortunate enough to be in her life.
*[*Type? Is that still even a word?]*

March 26

**<u>Hebrews 4:14-16</u>** (NIV) [14]*Therefore, since we have a great high priest who has ascended into heaven, Jesus the Son of God, let us hold firmly to the faith we profess.* [15]*For we do not have a high priest who is unable to empathize with our weaknesses, but we have one who has been tempted in every way, just as we are—yet he did not sin.* [16]*Let us then approach God's throne of grace with confidence, so that we may receive mercy and find grace to help us in our time of need.*

I write in the margins of my Bible(s) all the time to help me understand a passage. The note I wrote regarding verse 14 is that the word "have" is in the present tense! What a joy and amazing blessing to HAVE Jesus Who experienced **all** we experience because He was fully human while on this earth. A God Who knows what it's like to be human. He became one of us so He could not only reach us with His words, but He could comfort us with the *knowing and understanding* of what it felt like to experience it. Never quit believing. Approach Him with confidence and receive mercy and find grace that only He can give in our time of need. How could these verses not be favorites? Holy moly, this is good stuff, y'all!

March 27

**<u>Psalm 147:11</u>** (NIV) *the Lord delights in those who fear him, who put their hope in his unfailing love.*

This favorite verse reminds me that I/we have a Source of Strength to keep me/us out of the pit when life turns ugly on me/us. The note in the margin of my Bible regarding the word “fear” is respect or worship. When tragedy strikes, those of us with a firm faith in God are able to recognize and receive His love even in the midst of the hurricane of events blowing through our lives at the time. He delights in us and WILL sustain us through whatever our new normal may be.

March 28

**Luke 6:43-45** (NIV) [43]*"No good tree bears bad fruit, nor does a bad tree bear good fruit.* [44]*Each tree is recognized by its own fruit. People do not pick figs from thornbushes, or grapes from briers.* [45]*A good man brings good things out of the good stored up in his heart, and an evil man brings evil things out of the evil stored up in his heart. For the mouth speaks what the heart is full of."*

Whoa! This passage struck a chord with me as I struggled with anger, hurt, disappointment and a myriad of other emotions in the chapter of my life that I found myself. I realized after reading this new favorite passage how negatively I was allowing the situation to affect me. My heart was bubbling like a boiling pot with negative and unhealthy emotions. The words "acknowledge" (head) versus "act" (heart) are written in the margin of my Bible for verse 45b. Also written is a reference to Matthew 22:37 *Jesus replied: "'Love the Lord your God with all your heart and with all your soul and with all your mind'."* These verses reminded me that in the middle of the storms of life I must remain focused on God, loving Him with all my heart, soul, and mind in order to keep good, not evil, in my heart.

March 29

**Psalm 119:105-111** (CSB) *[105]Your word is a lamp for my feet, and a light on my path. [106]I have solemnly sworn to keep your righteous judgments. [107]I am severely afflicted; Lord, give me life according to your word. [108]Lord, please accept my freewill offerings of praise, and teach me your judgments. [109]My life is constantly in danger, yet I not do forget your instruction. [110]The wicked have set a trap for me, but I have not wandered from your precepts. [111]I have your decrees as a heritage forever; indeed, they are the joy of my heart.*

These favorite verses bring me back to my commitment to God, and how I walk with Him through the course of my life. They are the reminder and the staple of my faith. They bathe me in the fact that this is my heritage from generations before me, and it is my responsibility to share this with my children and their children in order for them to have this heritage for generations to come. Can I get an amen?

March 30

**Romans 7:14-25** (MSG) [14-16]*I can anticipate the response that is coming: "I know that all God's commands are spiritual, but I'm not. Isn't this also your experience?" Yes. I'm full of myself—after all, I've spent a long time in sin's prison. What I don't understand about myself is that I decide one way, but then I act another, doing things I absolutely despise. So if I can't be trusted to figure out what is best for myself and then do it, it becomes obvious that God's command is necessary.* [17-20]*But I need something more! For if I know the law but still can't keep it, and if the power of sin within me keeps sabotaging my best intentions, I obviously need help! I realize that I don't have what it takes. I can will it, but I can't do it. I decide to do good, but I don't really do it; I decide not to do bad, but then I do it anyway. My decisions, such as they are, don't result in actions. Something has gone wrong deep within me and gets the better of me every time.* [21-23]*It happens so regularly that it's predictable. The moment I decide to do good, sin is there to trip me up. I truly delight in God's commands, but it's pretty obvious that not all of me joins in that delight. Parts of me covertly rebel, and just when I least expect it, they take charge.* [24]*I've tried everything and nothing helps. I'm at the end of my rope. Is there no one who can do anything for me? Isn't that the real question?* [25]*The answer, thank God, is that Jesus Christ can and does. He acted to set things right in this life of contradictions where I want to serve God with all my heart and mind, but am pulled by the influence of sin to do something totally different.*

This favorite passage humbles me to know that St. Paul had the exact same issues as me. I want to do good I want to do what's right, and yet I mess up frequently. In the past several months I've gained extra pounds due to unhealthy food choices and little to no exercise. NO EXCUSES, it's on me (literally, my hips are bigger). And as I sat down for my devotion this morning, God led me to this passage. Of course, it's not just the unhealthy choices in my life that I'm talking about. That's just one current example. There are many times in my life, I find myself doing exactly the opposite of what I know to be the right thing. Praise be to God He isn't finished with me yet, and I continue to grow in His love and patience. I'm not positive but I think the word "patience" was first uttered as God finished molding me in my mother's womb… just sayin'.

March 31

**<u>Psalm 84:10-12</u>** (NIV) [10]*Better is one day in your courts than a thousand elsewhere; I would rather be a doorkeeper in the house of my God than dwell in the tents of the wicked.* [11]*For the Lord God is a sun and shield; the Lord bestows favor and honor; no good thing does he withhold from those whose walk is blameless.* [12]*Lord Almighty, blessed is the one who trusts in you.*

God is so good, and He blesses us all with His good gifts. It is such an honor to serve Him and to be in His Presence. This favorite passage just reminds me of what a joy it is to have a personal God Who is with us always. He shields us, He doesn't withhold good from us, and by the blood of Christ, we are blameless before Him. I am so grateful for the blessedness of serving the living God.

April 1

**Romans 8:1-6** (CSB) [1]*Therefore, there is now no condemnation for those in Christ Jesus,*[2] *because the law of the Spirit of life in Christ Jesus has set you free from the law of sin and death.* [3] *What the law could not do since it was weakened by the flesh, God did. He condemned sin in the flesh by sending his own Son in the likeness of sinful flesh as a sin offering,* [4] *in order that the law's requirement would be fulfilled in us who do not walk according to the flesh but according to the Spirit.* [5] *For those who live according to the flesh have their minds set on the things of the flesh but those who live according to the Spirit have their minds set on the things of the Spirit.* [6]*Now the mind-set of the flesh is death, but the mind-set of the Spirit is life and peace.*

I have two comments written in the margin of my Bible beside this favorite passage: 1) "yield to the Holy Spirit" and 2) "submerge ourselves in the Word". When I actually DO those two things, I KNOW I'm living the life Christ would have me live, and that it is possible to do so through His death and resurrection. The problem is, I don't always do those two things. I then find myself floundering. As I wrote that sentence the thought came to mind that a fish struggling out of water is similar to a Christian struggling when they aren't living in the Word. That's pretty simple stuff, y'all. No fooling!

April 2

**Jeremiah 18:1-6** (CSB) [1]*This is the word that came to Jeremiah from theLORD:* [2]*"Go down to the potter's house; there I will reveal my words to you."* [3]*So I went down to the potter's house, and there he was working away at the wheel.*[4]*But the jar that he was making from the clay became flawed in the potter's hand, so he made it into another jar, as it seemed right for him to do.* [5]*The word of the LORD came to me:* [6]*"House of Israel, can I not treat you as this potter treats his clay?" – this is the Lord's declaration. "Just like clay in the potter's hand, so are you in my hand, House of Israel."*

What a beautiful analogy of a potter remolding a piece of clay into something beautiful after something horrible has happened! The first time I read this passage it became a favorite. That is exactly what God can and does do with all of us. He takes the rubble of our lives and remolds us into something wonderful. This passage IS MY FAITH WALK. Remolding me from what I've been to what I can be is a full-time job for God. Thankfully, He's patient…just sayin'.

April 3

**Matthew 6:9-13** (KJV) [9]*After this manner therefore pray ye: Our Father which art in heaven, Hallowed be thy name.* [10]*Thy kingdom come, Thy will be done in earth, as it is in heaven.* [11]*Give us this day our daily bread.* [12]*And forgive us our debts, as we forgive our debtors.* [13]*And lead us not into temptation, but deliver us from evil: For thine is the kingdom, and the power, and the glory, forever. Amen.*

I learned this favorite passage using a KJV Bible, but somewhere along the way "debts/debtors" became "trespasses/trespassers". I'm guessing it's because it's easier to flow off the tongue when praying as a group in church, or maybe it's that *trespasses* encompass everything whereas *debts* may be construed as just financial issues. At any rate, the message from Jesus is the same – forgiveness. Many of us know that is much easier said than done. The point of this passage is how to pray. John Wesley suggested we pray this prayer daily. Pastor Dr. David Campbell, preached an entire series on this prayer, breaking down each phrase, and totally changing our lives. God's name is to be hallowed. He is the Sovereign God of the universe. We are His kingdom on earth and should live as such. Can you imagine the change we could make in the world? Daily bread – not just for us, but that which we share with others. Let God **lead** us and **deliver** us. God is the Power and Glory forever! He also suggested we pray it every day for 30 days and see the difference in our lives. As I write this, that was almost a year ago, and I'm still praying this prayer daily. I end my devotional time with this prayer, and my heart feels more prepared for worship – more prepared for life. As the kids told Mikey, "Try it, you'll like it."

April 4

**Psalm 32:5-8** (NIV) [5] *Then I acknowledged my sin to you and did not cover up my iniquity. I said, "I will confess my transgressions to the LORD." And you forgave the guilt of my sin.* [6] *Therefore let all the faithful pray to you while you may be found; surely the rising of the mighty waters will not reach them.* [7] *You are my hiding place; you will protect me from trouble and surround me with songs of deliverance.* [8] *I will instruct you and teach you in the way you should go; I will counsel you with my loving eye on you.*

As I mentioned in the foreword, we can read the same passage on different days and receive a new message! That's exactly what happened to me as I was gathering devotional information for this book. I first journaled this favorite passage on February 10, 2012. On that day, verse 8 (which is God speaking) jumped out at me and I wrote: **This passage hit me squarely between my two eyes, reminding me to take precious time to spend with God. Things – work, plans, life – will fall into place as a result of the time spent in worship and communication with God.** Almost three years to the day (February 14, 2015), and a few tragedies later, I read the passage again. This time verse 7 jumped out at me and I wrote: **This passage came on my radar and touched me as I dealt with Gail's loss once again as jury selection begins Thursday for the fourth suspect in her murder. Still praying he'll plead guilty like the others did and avoid the ordeal of a trial.** Gail was one of my younger sisters, and she was murdered in October 2012. My family and I had been through a lot in those three years, and God gave me the same passage with two different emphases: In 2012, reminding me to draw closer to Him and learn because He KNEW what was down the road for me and my family; In 2015 He KNEW my heart was breaking all over again as the looming trial brought all the details of October 2012, speeding back into our lives. And He assured me (and my family) that He would surround us. THAT is Who our God is! THAT is WHAT our God does!

April 5

**2 Timothy 1:12** (NIV) *That is why I am suffering as I am. Yet this is no cause for shame, because I know whom I have believed, and am convinced that he is able to guard what I have entrusted to him until that day.*

In order to know anyone, we must take the time to engage/visit/sit with that person. The same is true of God. To KNOW Him, we must engage/visit/sit with Him, too! We do all this as we read His Word, as we talk with Him in prayer and as we listen to Him in meditation. As we study and research questions we have, using various translations and/or other Bible guides, we also learn more about God and His Word. Thankfully, we don't suffer for worshipping God, but in some other countries, people are not free to worship as we are. In Biblical days, Christians suffered for believing. Even though this letter is written specifically to Timothy, Paul is giving us all encouragement to remain strong in our beliefs. This favorite verse reminds me to KNOW Whom I have believed, to live my life accordingly, and to remain strong and firm in my beliefs. Can I get an amen?

April 6

**<u>Psalm 130: 3-4</u>** (NLT) [3] *LORD, if you kept a record of our sins, who, O Lord, could ever survive?* [4] *But you offer forgiveness, that we might learn to fear you.*

Verses that reference fearing God need to be interpreted as revering, honoring, respecting, or reverencing. All the positive words mold God into our heart and lives. Fear to me is only to the extent most children fear a parent – not in a negative sense, but in a respectful sense. We give Him honor and praise. We revere Him. We respect Him. We obey Him because we LOVE Him. I heard a sermon once, comparing our love to God to our dog's love for us. Our dogs obey us because they love us. This favorite verse is a reminder of God's forgiveness and love for us, and in turn our love and devotion to Him. Can I get a bow-wow, I mean an amen?

April 7

**Proverbs 16:23-24** (NIV) [23]*The hearts of the wise make their mouths prudent, and their lips promote instruction.* [24]*Gracious words are a honeycomb, sweet to the soul and healing to the bones.*

These verses are favorites because they help me keep my mouth under control – most of the time. Trust me, it's more often than it used to be, but I'm still working on it. Wisdom in the Lord allows us to step back before we speak (that's what I'm still working on). Even when we are upset, if we take a minute, we can then speak respectfully, allowing us to diffuse a situation. Then we may have a healing effect on the people involved as well as the situation itself. To those that know me well, I'm getting better at this, right, y'all? Y'all?

April 8

**<u>Psalm 116:1-7</u>** (NLT) [1] *I love the LORD because he hears my voice and my prayer for mercy.* [2] *Because he bends down to listen, I will pray as long as I have breath!* [3] *Death wrapped its ropes around me; the terrors of the grave overtook me. I saw only trouble and sorrow.* [4] *Then I called on the name of the LORD: "Please, LORD, save me!"* [5] *How kind the LORD is! How good he is! So merciful, this God of ours!*
[6]*The LORD protects those of childlike faith; I was facing death, and he saved me.* [7] *Let my soul be at rest again, for the LORD has been good to me.*

Verse 2 reminds me of how we converse with toddlers. We squat down so we're on their level. That's what Jesus did when He left Heaven to be on our level and live as one of us. He squatted down and spoke to us. That is just beautiful to me, hence another favorite verse. Doesn't it just give you chills? The God of the universe takes time to bend down and listen to us! O, that we would look up and listen to Him.

April 9

**Philippians 2:13** (NIV) *for it is God who works in you to will and to act in order to fulfill his good purpose.*

God works in us to guide our will and our actions – we must be receptive of Him and His Presence in our lives each and every day. Each and every moment, each and every situation. Feeling His Presence is the most awesome and incredible experience a Christian can have. The perfect peace of God flowing in you as you move about the day-to-day tasks of this life will be all the strength you ever need. This favorite verse speaks of that beautifully.

April 10

**<u>Psalm 104:33</u>** (NIV) *I will sing to the LORD all my life; I will sing praise to my God as long as I live.*

I love how the Psalmist wrote exactly what I feel that happens so often if you open yourself up for the surprise of the moment from God. I will sing and praise Him all the days of my life. Of course, this is a favorite verse because music is an important part of my life. God has put a song in my heart – no doubt. And that beautiful music rings loudly and clearly as I navigate this thing we call life.

April 11

**2 Timothy 3:1-5** (NIV) [1] *But mark this: There will be terrible times in the last days.* [2] *People will be lovers of themselves, lovers of money, boastful, proud, abusive, disobedient to their parents, ungrateful, unholy,* [3] *without love, unforgiving, slanderous, without self-control, brutal, not lovers of the good,* [4] *treacherous, rash, conceited, lovers of pleasure rather than lovers of God—* [5] *having a form of godliness but denying its power. Have nothing to do with such people.*

This favorite verse is quite clear and could have been written in the *Marietta Daily Journal* this morning! So many people are caught up in the ways of the world with little or no thought to God and His love, purpose, or plans for us. May those of us who embrace the love and power that is ours through Him, share it with a sick and dying world. And I don't mean by cramming our beliefs down their throats. I mean by living in a such a way that they'll ask us, "what is the difference?", "how do you maneuver life with joy?" And we can respond, "by the love and care of God, through Jesus Christ, His Son, our Lord!" Amen!

April 12

Beginning today through April 16th we'll be taking one of my favorite Psalms (103) and digesting portions of it each day using the New Living Translation.

**Psalm 103: 1-2** (NLT) [1] *Let all that I am praise the LORD; with my whole heart, I will praise his holy name.* [2] *Let all that I am praise the LORD; may I never forget the good things he does for me.*

These favorite verses remind me to not only praise God for what He has done, but also to be mindful enough to recognize them! I sometimes get so busy I don't even see my blessings, let alone acknowledge them. That is not acceptable, y'all. We should always be aware of God and His workings in our lives. Thank Him every day for the miracles of our lives. Can I get a witness?

April 13

**Psalm 103:3-5** (NLT) [3] *He forgives all my sins and heals all my diseases.* [4] *He redeems me from death and crowns me with love and tender mercies.* [5] *He fills my life with good things. My youth is renewed like the eagle's!*

What great verses for my first 10K in years! The date was March 28, 2015, and we were doing the Cooper Bridge Run, in Charleston, SC. Not only is this a 10K, but part of the race is run over a 2-mile extension bridge with a very high peak in the middle of it! My distresses would be the little aches and pains along the way, and a little trouble breathing up that high peak. I renew my youth by staying fit and participating in races, even if I mostly walk, rather than run. Beyond the race, my distresses are all the curve balls life sends my way. And forgiveness? I need it every day – and, praise God He forgives and loves me always, in spite of myself. No wonder these are favorite verses of mine!

April 14

**Psalm 103:6-9** (NLT) *[6]The LORD gives righteousness and justice to all who are treated unfairly. [7]He revealed his character to Moses and his deeds to the people of Israel. [8]The LORD is compassionate and merciful, slow to get angry and filled with unfailing love. [9]He will not constantly accuse us, nor remain angry forever.*

Comforting verses like these are always favorites for me. I find such peace in reading them. This passage details the patience and love God has toward us even when we make mistakes – which for me is constantly. It also speaks of hope and His compassion for those who are mistreated. It's not enough to just sympathize or empathize with those hurting; it's not enough to see a wrong, and comment "that's not right". We need to DO something. God DID something – He created us! We are His hands and feet on this earth. Now, let's get busy living for God, y'all!

April 15

**Psalm 103:10-18** (NLT) [10] *He does not punish us for all our sins; he does not deal harshly with us, as we deserve.* [11] *For his unfailing love toward those who fear him is as great as the height of the heavens above the earth.* [12] *He has removed our sins as far from us as the east is from the west.* [13] *The LORD is like a father to his children, tender and compassionate to those who fear him.* [14] *For he knows how weak we are; he remembers we are only dust.* [15] *Our days on earth are like grass; like wildflowers, we bloom and die.* [16] *The wind blows, and we are gone — as though we had never been here.* [17] *But the love of the LORD remains forever with those who fear him. His salvation extends to the children's children* [18] *of those who are faithful to his covenant, of those who obey his commandments!*

These favorite verses speak of God's patience with us and I am so thankful for that, as I'm sure I try His patience on a daily basis. The passage compares Him to a loving father who is tender and compassionate. The word fear, as I've mentioned before, is meant here as respect. I can relate to that usage here because I remember as a child having a certain fear of not wanting to disappoint my parents.

April 16

**Psalm 103:19-22** (NLT) [19] *The LORD has made the heavens his throne; from there he rules over everything.* [20] *Praise the LORD, you angels, you mighty ones who carry out his plans, listening for each of his commands.* [21] *Yes, praise the LORD, you armies of angels who serve him and do his will!* [22] *Praise the LORD, everything he has created, everything in all his kingdom. Let all that I am praise the LORD.*

These favorite verses speak to me of the sovereignty of God. He is on His throne. He IS God, and we are not. Every fiber of my being should exalt and praise Him! I reflect on times my quick temper has gotten - and occasionally still gets - in the way of that. For the most part, my temper is kept at bay with regard to face-to-face confrontations, and I thank God for His guidance in that area of my personality. Now if I could just stay calm during athletic events where the referees/ umpires/officials (pick one) just blatantly get it wrong – or in Atlanta rush hour… sigh. I humbly pray for God to continue to guide me toward a personality not so quick to anger, and in a direction that will utilize that energy for the good of His Kingdom.

April 17

**<u>2 Timothy 2:1</u>** (NIV) *You then, my son, be strong in the grace that is in Christ Jesus.*

My prayer is that our Father, God, will help me stay strong in Him – moving in and breathing out his love and mercy. Sometimes life seems hard and our stress level is just “off the charts”. That’s when we tend to call on God; however, how much better would it be if we lived our lives in such a way that we always in tune with God’s love and mercy. That is my goal, and this favorite verse helps keep me focused.

April 18

**Isaiah 6:8** (NIV) *Then I heard the voice of the Lord saying, "Whom shall I send? And who will go for us?" And I said, "Here am I. Send me!"*

I absolutely love this verse! It touches my heart now just as it did the first time I ever read it. Just because we don't go to the ends of the earth as missionaries, doesn't mean we can't be about God's work right where we are. God can and will use us if we are open to the challenge, and to His Word. This favorite verse places on my heart to be the hands and feet of Jesus. Everywhere. Anywhere. Anytime. Always. Can I get an amen?

April 19

**Matthew 24:14** (NIV) *And this gospel of the kingdom will be preached in the whole world as a testimony to all nations, and then the end will come.*

These are the words of Jesus. It is up to us to continue the Word on earth and do our part to ensure everyone hears. And not only HEARS, but also SEES IN US the Love of God! We can talk about God/Jesus/Love from sun up to sun down, but if people don't see our faith in our daily walk all our words fall on deaf ears and are just hot air. Our lives MUST reflect the difference God makes in us! My prayer is that, even with all my shortcomings, I reflect God's Love. This favorite verse reminds me I am part of God's kingdom, and as such I'm responsible for spreading the gospel as a testimony to what He means in my life.

April 20

**Psalm 86:7** (MSG) *Every time I'm in trouble I call on you, confident that you'll answer.*

I love the way The Message uses the words "confident that You'll answer" in this favorite verse. That is faith! I learned over 40 years ago that the "answer" is not always "yes". God also answers with "no" and sometimes "wait". Regardless of the answer, I KNOW – I am confident – that God WILL answer and that He will be with us through whatever we face. A person much wiser than me once said "prayer doesn't change things, it changes you". When I call on God during the trouble, the trouble may be unchanged and still be there – but so is God – and, as a result, I'm changed.

April 21

**<u>Psalm 18:2, 6</u>** (NIV) [2]*The LORD is my rock, my fortress and my deliverer; my God is my rock, in whom I take refuge, my shield and the horn of my salvation, my stronghold.* [6] *In my distress I called to the LORD; I cried to my God for help. From his temple he heard my voice; my cry came before him, into his ears.*

These became favorite verses on February 12, 2015, when jury selection was to begin in the trial of the 4th and final person responsible for my sister's murder. What appropriate verses they were, as I was needing comfort, strength, and refuge in the strong and loving arms of my Lord! That's the way God works: leading us to just the verses we need at just the times we need them. What an awesome and loving God we serve!

April 22

**Psalm 78:1-7** (CSB) *[1]My people, hear my instruction; listen to the words from my mouth. [2]I will declare my sayings; I will speak mysteries from the past—[3]things we have heard and known and that our fathers have passed down to us. [4]We will not hide them from their children, but will tell a future generation the praiseworthy acts of the LORD, his might, and the wondrous works he has performed. [5]He established a testimony in Jacob and set up a law in Israel, which he commanded our fathers to teach to their children [6]so that a future generation – children yet to be born – might know. They were to rise and tell their children [7]so that they might put their confidence in God and not forget God's works, but keep his commands.*

As I was searching through my journals for entries to include in this book, I ran across my entry of December 19, 2010, which was the first time one of our grandchildren was old enough to read the Christmas story from the Bible. I was all excited about our new tradition and wrote, "a little child shall lead them", quoting a well-known scripture. At the time, I hadn't researched that verse. When I looked it up today, I realized I'd used it out of context. The verse is Isaiah 11:6, but it's talking about the Peace we'll have on earth when Christ reigns, not about a little child leading us. The message I want to share now from this favorite passage is that we MUST pass our faith onto our children and grandchildren by sharing with them what we know of God. Sharing with them what He means to us. Let them see God living in us. It's also a good idea to be sure the verse(s) we quote are in context – just sayin'.

April 23

**Psalm 70** (MSG) [1-3]*God! Please hurry to my rescue! GOD, come quickly to my side! Those who are out to get me—let them fall all over themselves. Those who relish my downfall—send them down a blind alley. Give them a taste of their own medicine, those gossips off clucking their tongues.* [4]*Let those on the hunt for you sing and celebrate. Let all who love your saving way say over and over, "God is mighty!"* [5]*But I've lost it. I'm wasted. God—quickly, quickly! Quick to my side, quick to my rescue! GOD, don't lose a minute.*

The first time I remember this favorite passage resonating with me was in January 2010, when I was in the middle of a family crisis. A friend walked into my office one day with her Bible and said, "I have the perfect Scripture for you," and proceeded to read Psalm 70 from The Message. Through the years since, I have often revisited this passage. I'm sure it resonates with most people at one time or another. I love the way The Message reads, but it's a beautiful and meaningful passage no matter what translation you prefer. David cried out to God, who listened and brought comfort – we cry out to God, who listens and brings comfort.

April 24

<u>**Matthew 1:18-25**</u> (CSB) [18]*The birth of Jesus Christ came about this way: After his mother Mary had been engaged to Joseph, it was discovered before they came together that she was pregnant from the Holy Spirit.* [19]*So her husband Joseph, being righteous man, and not wanting to disgrace her publicly, decided to divorce her secretly.* [20]*But after he had considered these things, an angel of the Lord appeared to him in a dream saying, "Joseph, son of David, don't be afraid to take Mary as your wife, because what has been conceived in her is from the Holy Spirit.* [21]*She will give birth to a son, and you are to name him Jesus, because he will save his people from their sins."* [22]*Now all this took place to fulfill what was spoken by the Lord through the prophet:* [23]***See the virgin will become pregnant and give birth to a son, and they will name him Immanuel,*** *which is translated "God is with us."* [24]*When Joseph woke up, he did as the Lord's angel had commanded him. He married her but did not have sexual relations with her until she gave birth to a son. And he named him Jesus.*

Mary and Joseph both trusted God with a seemingly impossible, implausible happening. God was, and is, in control. He sent Jesus to save us from our sins and to be with us – Immanuel, God with us – right here, right now. In the above favorite passage, Joseph accepts Jesus as his earthly son and rears Him as if He were his son. Jesus grew up just like any other boy of His day, with one **huge** exception – He was fully human, AND fully God. We are to accept Him as our Lord and Savior and trust Him in the seemingly impossible and implausible happenings in our lives.

April 25

**Psalm 16:7-9** (NIV) [7]*I will praise the LORD, who counsels me; even at night my heart instructs me.* [8]*I keep my eyes always on the LORD. With him at my right hand, I will not be shaken.* [9]*Therefore my heart is glad and my tongue rejoices; my body also will rest secure.*

These favorite verses speak to me of the assurance we have when we rest in God. When we allow Him to be our focus, we are not shaken by life's curve balls. Our hearts are glad and joyful regardless of our circumstances. The last sentence of verse 9 brought to mind how I envision crawling into God's lap to find my peace. I've done that often through the years.

April 26

**2 Kings 2:1-6** (CSB) [1]*The time had come from the Lord to take Elijah up to heaven in a whirlwind. Elijah and Elisha were traveling from Gilgal,* [2]*and Elijah said to Elisha, "Stay here; the* LORD *is sending me to Bethel." But Elisha replied, "As the* LORD *lives and as you yourself live, I will not leave you." So they went down to Bethel.* [3]*Then the sons of the prophets who were at Bethel came out to Elisha and said, "Do you know that the* LORD *will take your master away from you today?" He said, "Yes, I know. Be quiet."* [4]*Elijah said to him, "Elisha, stay here; the* LORD *is sending me to Jericho." But Elisha said, "As the* LORD *lives and as you yourself live, I will not leave you." So they went to Jericho.* [5]*Then the sons of the prophets who were in Jericho came out to Elisha and said, "Do you know that the* LORD *will take your master away from you today?" He said, "Yes, I know. Be quiet."* [6]*Elijah said to him, "Stay here; the* LORD *is sending me to the Jordan." But Elisha said, "As the* LORD *lives and as you yourself live, I will not leave you." So the two of them went on.*

When I initially read this passage, the message I was to receive was not clear to me at all. I planned to read something else later after work that evening. Before I had the chance to do that, I received the phone call from my best friend's husband saying she had gone to be with Jesus. Iris had been sick for many years battling early onset Alzheimer's. She was only 58. I didn't read another passage that evening, but the next morning the above passage meant something to me and became a favorite. When a Christian leaves this world, they leave enough of themselves through the life they've lived and what they've taught us, for the rest of us to carry on. Iris touched not only my life, but everyone with whom she came in contact. We are all better people for having known her and learning of her faith. We now need to share our faith, just as she shared hers.

April 27

**<u>Psalm 8:3-5</u>** (NIV) [3]*When I consider your heavens, the work of your fingers, the moon and the stars, which you have set in place,* [4]*what is mankind that you are mindful of them, human beings that you care for them?* [5]*You have made them a little lower than the angels and crowned them with glory and honor.*

This favorite passage causes me to stop and reflect on all God's creations. The heavens, the moon and stars – all set in place just right. One of my favorite places to contemplate and slow down is my deck at night. I stare up into the night sky and the twinkling stars seem to play God's love, peace and strength to me as if it were a hymn. And then I catch my breath because in all this beauty and majesty, HE LOVES ME.

April 28

**Revelation 1:17** (NIV) *When I saw him, I fell at his feet as though dead. Then he placed his right hand on me and said: "Do not be afraid. I am the First and the Last."*

Describing the risen Christ cannot be done with the words we know. God cannot be contained on a written page. We fall down before Him and He touches us – and we are never the same again. And we try so hard to pinpoint and say exactly what He means to us, and how His love infuses us, and we fall so short. My prayer is that my life be a beacon and a representation of Christ in me for all to see. This favorite verse touches me deeply. It reminds me of the song *I Can Only Imagine* about what it will be like seeing God/Jesus for the first time.

[Author's note: My favorite rendition of the song is by the gospel group Mercy Me, featuring Trace Adkins.]

April 29

**Psalm 66:16-20** (MSG) [16-20]*All believers, come here and listen, let me tell you what God did for me. I called out to him with my mouth, my tongue shaped the sounds of music. If I had been cozy with evil, the Lord would never have listened. But he most surely did listen, he came on the double when he heard my prayer. Blessed be God: he didn't turn a deaf ear, he stayed with me, loyal in his love.*

God does NOT cram Himself down our throats. He does not make us turn to Him. He waits patiently for us to repent of our sins and He's there for us totally and completely. I love the wording of this favorite passage, as it speaks of God listening and staying. How amazing is that? The God of the universe listening and staying for me – for y'all.

April 30

**Matthew 6:28-30** (NIV) [28]*"And why do you worry about clothes? See how the flowers of the field grow. They do not labor or spin.* [29]*Yet I tell you that not even Solomon in all his splendor was dressed like one of these.* [30]*If that is how God clothes the grass of the field, which is here today and tomorrow is thrown into the fire, will he not much more clothe you—you of little faith?*

We are so busy looking at all the things to distract us we fail to see the simple truths of God. This passage has been a favorite since my early teens. I'm 68 at this writing, so that's a LONG time. It hits the nail on the head, and it should hit us all OVER the head! God will take care of us! He takes care of the flowers and they surely do not worry and fret as we do. TRUST Him – He will NOT let you down. Can I get an amen?

May 1

**<u>Psalm 62:1-2</u>** (NIV) [1]*Truly my soul finds rest in God; my salvation comes from him.* [2]*Truly he is my rock and my salvation; he is my fortress, I will never be shaken.*

The first line of this favorite Psalm says it all for me. I DO find rest in God. A rest that is complete and total. A rest that soothes my weary soul. A rest that comforts my heart to its very core. A rest that is beyond my ability to fully express the magnitude of the peace I feel. Let us all rest in the Lord. Can I get an amen?

May 2

**Matthew 18:21-22** (NIV) [21]*Then Peter came to Jesus and asked, "Lord, how many times shall I forgive my brother or sister who sins against me? Up to seven times?"* [22]*Jesus answered, "I tell you, not seven times, but seventy-seven times."*

We are required to forgive others just as it is written in this favorite passage. I have the word "limitless" written in the margin of my Bible. However, forgiveness is NOT condoning, taking abuse, or enabling. It IS a matter of the heart – our very being. The love of God flows through us and, as a result we have the capacity to forgive. Forgiveness isn't for the person who has wronged us; forgiveness is for us. Forgiveness keeps us from becoming bitter, hateful, and miserable. Forgiveness keeps us living out our faith. Forgiveness is God's love.

May 3

**<u>Psalm 51:10</u>** (NIV) *Create in me a pure heart, O God, and renew a steadfast spirit within me.*

Sometimes I like to take a favorite verse like this one and compare different translations/versions. Occasionally, I've gotten a completely different meaning and I must be honest, those times are very confusing to me. My rule of thumb is to allow God to point me to the version I need at the time. However, this verse is very plain and simple, but just for fun I decided to read the NLT and MSG, in addition to the NIV above

(NLT): *Create in me a clean heart, O God. Renew a loyal spirit within me.*

(MSG): *God, make a fresh start in me, shape a Genesis week from the chaos of my life.*

On days like this morning, I feel as if God is right here at the table having coffee with me. My heart and soul are renewed!

May 4

**<u>John 1:4-5</u>** (NIV) [4]*In him was life, and that life was the light of all mankind.* [5]*The light shines in the darkness, and the darkness has not overcome it.*

God's light shines even in the bad times – so don't grow weary and lose heart. Know and feel His Presence. Many, many times* in my life I've faced circumstances that I thought were the worst that could possibly happen to me, only later to learn there actually was something worse and it WAS happening to me! This favorite passage reminds me, through it all, no matter the pain, the turmoil, the devastation, God is there and His Light shines on my path.

*There are many times I could share, but one of those times was in 2006, when my best friend, Iris, and I sang a duet in her church in Union, SC. She had recently been diagnosed with Early Onset Alzheimer's, and we both knew our lives had been changed forever. Yet, because of our faith we were able to sing the gospel song, <u>Through It All.</u> We sang loudly and clearly that day "through it all, I've learned to trust in Jesus, I've learned to trust in God." Amen.

May 5

**<u>Psalm 25:4-5, 15</u>** (NLT) [4]*Show me the right path, O* L*ORD; point out the road for me to follow.* [5]*Lead me by your truth and teach me, for you are the God who saves me. All day long I put my hope in you.* [15]*My eyes are always on the* LORD, *for he rescues me from the traps of my enemies.*

The way God leads me to verses continues to amaze me. After a very trying few days, what an amazing passage to read and, as a result, I have a new favorite passage! Life is not easy. As the old country song says, we're not promised a rose garden. There are forces everywhere trying to trip us up, break us, yea verily, destroy us. King David's life was no different than ours. Just like us, outside forces were fighting him, family members were fighting him, and he was messing up a great deal all on his own. I don't know about you, but that pretty much describes my life. In spite of the life we're dealt, or the life we create due to our own missteps, God WILL show us the right path. He WILL lead our way. He WILL rescue us.

May 6

**<u>Hebrews 12:2</u>** (NIV) *our eyes on Jesus, the pioneer and perfecter of faith. For the joy set before him he endured the cross, scorning its shame, and sat down at the right hand of the throne of God.*

Fix your eyes upon Jesus and trust Him to walk with you holding your hand, and carrying you when necessary. I learned a long time ago that if I want to cut fabric or wrapping paper straight, I must **not** look at the scissors, but at the place I'm wanting to end at (yikes, a preposition at the end of a sentence – nope, I added a parenthesis ha, ha). When I look at the scissors, the line I cut looks like a crooked country road; when I look at the place I'm heading with the scissors, the line is straight. The same holds true for our faith journey. If our eyes are set on Christ, as this favorite verse says, our journey will be meaningful, regardless of what we encounter along the way.

May 7

**Psalm 19:14** (NLT) *May the words of my mouth and the meditation of my heart be pleasing to you, O LORD, my rock and my redeemer.*

I am so guilty of letting the unimportant, everyday trials of life knock God right off the throne of my life in the heat of the moment. I've known this favorite verse since I was a child, and yet things like someone cutting me off in traffic rile me up. You'd think I'd be used to this, living in Atlanta! An awful and wrong call by an umpire or referee during a ball game has been known to make my blood boil, and as a result I've acted in an unholy fashion. When did I allow this to enter my heart? When will I do something about it? How about now?

May 8

**<u>Ephesians 3:20-21</u>** (NIV)[20]*Now to him who is able to do immeasurably more than all we ask or imagine, according to his power that is at work within us,* [21]*to him be glory in the church and in Christ Jesus throughout all generations, for ever and ever! Amen.*

We should bring all our weaknesses to Christ and He will give us strength. I don't remember when I first heard/read this passage, but early on it became a favorite because it's my faith in a nutshell. God is alive and well, and working in our lives constantly. We need to attune ourselves with what He is already doing. He is our Shepherd and will protect us. Rest in Him. Christ is so strong in our weaknesses.

May 9

**Psalm 42:5** (NIV) *Why, my soul, are you downcast? Why so disturbed within me? Put your hope in God, for I will yet praise him, my Savior and my God.*

This is the verse I read on February 19, 2015, as our family approached what was supposed to be the trial for the fourth and final defendant in the murder of my sister, Gail. For days God had been preparing our family, serving up Scriptures to all of us. My sister, Jo Ellen, and I were sharing the verses on our Facebook pages. This is what I wrote in my journal on that day: **The verses coming to my heart this week, as well as those I'm finding on Jo Ellen's Facebook page, are speaking to me so clearly as we move toward the trial that shouldn't be. I've spent so much time over the past several days wishing it wasn't happening* rather than holding God's Hand and saying, "Let's do this".** As I sit here now, writing this book, this favorite verse continues to speak to my soul and give me peace.

[*I just wanted him to plead guilty.]

May 10

**Psalm 37:4** (NIV) *Take delight in the LORD, and he will give you the desires of your heart.*

Emanuel – God with us. And He is – day and night, 24/7 – moving, breathing, walking, carrying His children. So many times in my life I've felt I couldn't put one foot in front of the other, and yet, I did. How? God was with me and helped me over, around, or through whatever was happening at the time – divorce, death of loved ones, illness (my own or a loved one's), murder, car wreck, moving to another state, debt – you name it, God has helped me through it! We are so blessed to have Scripture filled with favorite verses like this one that we can call to mind as needed on this journey we call life. Amen and Amen.

May 11

**Psalm 119:11, 18** (NLT) [11]*I have hidden your word in my heart, that I might not sin against you.* [18]*Open my eyes to see the wonderful truths in your instructions.*

Two beautiful favorite verses reminding me to keep God's Word close to my heart. To ask for His help enabling me to SEE (truly SEE) the marvelous truths He has provided through His Word. When we open our eyes to God's truths, y'all, it's like opening a window in our house and allowing the sunshine in. That reminds me of our cat, Molly, who will lay down in any sunlight she finds coming through our windows. She just soaks it up in utter silence. That's what we should do with God's Word. When I lay in the sunlight of God's Word, and soak it up in the quietness of just being, I feel His Light all the way to my soul!

May 12

**John 6:35** (NIV) *Then Jesus declared, "I am the bread of life. Whoever comes to me will never go hungry, and whoever believes in me will never be thirsty."*

Jesus is our food and our drink. When we feast in Him, we have all we need. Everything. He declared that in this favorite verse! It wasn't just a comment in passing, it was a declaration! There are several times in Scripture where we see the words "I AM". The first time is in Exodus 3:14, when God says to Moses, "This is what you say to the Israelite: 'I AM has sent me to you'." Jesus is the great I AM, and He is all we need, y'all. He's all we need.

May 13

**Psalm 122** (CSB) [1]*I rejoiced with those who said to me, "Let us go to the house of the LORD."* [2]*Our feet were standing within your gates, Jerusalem --* [3]*Jerusalem, built as a city should be, solidly united,* [4]*where the tribes, the Lord's tribes, go up to give thanks to the name of the LORD. (This is an ordinance for Israel.)* [5]*There, thrones for judgment are placed, thrones of the house of David.* [6]*Pray for the well-being of Jerusalem: "May those who love you be secure;* [7]*may there be peace within your walls, security within your fortresses."* [8]*Because of my brothers and friends, I will say, "May peace be in you."* [9]*Because of the house of the LORD our God, I will pursue your prosperity.*

The peace that comes from God is so wonderful – like sunshine on your face or the warmth of a shower when you've come in from the cold. No words adequately nor completely describe it because it does *pass all understanding.* This favorite Psalm was written straight from King David's heart. Having visited Jerusalem, this Psalm has taken on even more meaning to me, as I walked where King David walked. He was a man with flaws just like us, and yet he was SO in-tune with God that the words he wrote centuries ago comfort and guide those of us who read them. Peace indeed, peace indeed.

May 14

**<u>Matthew 18:2-5</u>** (NIV) [2]*He called a little child to him, and placed the child among them.* [3]*And he said: "Truly I tell you, unless you change and become like little children, you will never enter the kingdom of heaven.* [4]*Therefore, whoever takes the lowly position of this child is the greatest in the kingdom of heaven.* [5]*And whoever welcomes one such child in my name welcomes me."*

Once we're grown, it's hard to remember *exactly* what it was like to be a kid. Oh, we have memories and joys of our childhood, but I'm talking about the unblemished outlook we had because we hadn't been exposed to things that would tarnish our view and make us cynical. We trusted!! We believed!! In this favorite passage, Jesus calls us to become as little children in order to embrace His kingdom and the ideologies that come with faith. Our eyes will see as children see. It is sinful for us to NOT see a true need because of pettiness or prejudice that blocks our view. Drop all that away and believe like a young child again. Let's worship God through the untainted glasses of a child. Can I get a witness?

May 15

**<u>Isaiah 56:4-7</u>** (NIV) [4]*For this is what the LORD says: "To the eunuchs who keep my Sabbaths, who choose what pleases me and hold fast to my covenant—*[5]*to them I will give within my temple and its walls a memorial and a name better than sons and daughters; I will give them an everlasting name that will endure forever.* [6]*And foreigners who bind themselves to the LORD to minister to him, to love the name of the LORD, and to be his servants, all who keep the Sabbath without desecrating it and who hold fast to my covenant—*[7]*these I will bring to my holy mountain and give them joy in my house of prayer. Their burnt offerings and sacrifices will be accepted on my altar; for my house will be called a house of prayer for all nations."*

As we go to God, He molds us into His sons and daughters, and we are given "an everlasting name that will not be cut off". This favorite passage assures us of that! His house shall be "called a house of prayer for all nations". When we were in Israel, we visited the Church of All Nations. I can't even describe what I felt there that day. A group of Koreans were ahead of us, and they stood outside this holy place praising God in their native tongue, and all we understood was "hallelujah" – hallelujah indeed, and amen. All people from all nations were there that day, worshipping One Lord, One God, Who IS the God of the universe forever and for all.

May 16

**Matthew 4:1-11** (MSG) [1-3] *Next Jesus was taken into the wild by the Spirit for the Test. The Devil was ready to give it. Jesus prepared for the Test by fasting forty days and forty nights. That left him, of course, in a state of extreme hunger, which the Devil took advantage of in the first test: "Since you are God's Son, speak the word that will turn these stones into loaves of bread."* [4]*Jesus answered by quoting Deuteronomy: "It takes more than bread to stay alive. It takes a steady stream of words from God's mouth."* [5-6]*For the second test the Devil took him into the Holy City. He sat him on top of the Temple and said, "Since you are God's Son, jump. The Devil goaded him by quoting Psalms 91: "He has placed you in the care of the angels. They will catch you so that you won't so much as stub your toe on a stone."* [7]*Jesus countered with another citation from Deuteronomy: "Don't you dare test the Lord your God."* [8-9]*For the third test, the Devil took him to the peak of a huge mountain. He gestured expansively, pointing out all the earth's kingdoms, how glorious they all were. Then he said, "They're yours – lock, stock, and barrel. Just go down on your knees and worship me, and they're yours."* [10]*Jesus' refusal was curt: "Beat it, Satan! He backed his rebuke with a third quotation from Deuteronomy: "Worship the Lord your God, and only him. Serve him with absolute single-heartedness."* [11]*The Test was over. The Devil left. And in his place, angels! Angels came and took care of Jesus' needs.*

The temptations of Christ cover ALL temptations we have had or will ever have. He proved humans *CAN* withstand temptation! This is why this passage is a favorite. The Spirit that led Christ into the wilderness is the Holy Spirit, who dwells in us and helps us through life. The very last temptation, verse 8, when Satan offers Him the world is such a wake-up call to me. There is NOTHING Satan can offer us that we don't already have over and above in Christ!! Jesus taught us that. May we all tap into the Power we have to overcome Satan.

May 17

**JOHN 16:22, 33** (NIV) [22] *So with you: Now is your time of grief, but I will see you again and you will rejoice, and no one will take away your joy.* [33] *"I have told you these things, so that in me you may have peace. In this world you will have trouble. But take heart! I have overcome the world."*

Favorite verses because they speak of grief in a very real and personal way. Jesus knew His death was imminent and that the disciples needed His Truth to cling to. Any of us who have lost loved ones or have someone in hospice now, know this. Rest in God's Presence. No matter what we are facing, no matter what happens, we will have Peace.

May 18

**<u>Isaiah 40:11, 53:3</u>** (NIV) [11] *He tends his flock like a shepherd: He gathers the lambs in his arms and carries them close to his heart; he gently leads those that have young.* [3] *He was despised and rejected by mankind, a man of suffering, and familiar with pain. Like one from whom people hide their faces he was despised, and we held him in low esteem.*

I don't know about you, but I've always loved and embraced the idea of Jesus being my Shepherd. It's no wonder that these two verses are favorites of mine. Jesus KNOWS and UNDERSTANDS suffering, so when we hurt it's easy for us to envision Him gathering us close and carrying us. He is the Someone who can feel what we feel. He also teaches us a better way, a new way to think and listen to our hearts so we are less likely to hurt one another, and more likely to help.

May 19

**John 4:1-26** (MSG) [1-3]*Jesus realized that the Pharisees were keeping count of the baptisms that he and John performed (although his disciples, not Jesus, did the actual baptizing). They had posted the score that Jesus was ahead, turning him and John into rivals in the eyes of the people. So Jesus left the Judean countryside and went back to Galilee.* [4-6] *To get there, he had to pass through Samaria. He came into Sychar, a Samaritan village that bordered the field Jacob had given to his son Joseph. Jacob's well was still there. Jesus, worn out by the trip, sat down at the well. It was noon.*[7-8] *A woman, a Samaritan, came to draw water. Jesus said, "Would you give me a drink of water?" (His disciples had gone to the village to buy food for lunch.)* [9]*The Samaritan woman, taken aback, asked, "How come you, a Jew, are asking me, a Samaritan woman, for a drink?" (Jews in those days wouldn't be caught dead talking to Samaritans.)* [10]*Jesus answered, "If you knew the generosity of God and who I am, you would be asking me for a drink, and I would give you fresh, living water."* [11-12]*The woman said, "Sir, you don't even have a bucket to draw with, and this well is deep. So how are you going to get this 'living water'? Are you a better man than our ancestor Jacob, who dug this well and drank from it, he and his sons and livestock, and passed it down to us?"* [13-14]*Jesus said, "Everyone who drinks this water will get thirsty again and again. Anyone who drinks the water I give will never thirst – not ever. The water I give will be an artisan spring within, gushing fountains of endless life."* [15]*The woman said, "Sir, give me this water so that I won't get thirsty, won't ever have to come back to this well again!"* [16]*He said, "Go call your husband and then come back."* [17-18]*"I have no husband," she said. "That's nicely put: 'I have no husband.' You've had five husbands, and the man you're living with now isn't even your husband. You spoke the truth there, sure* *enough." [19-20] "Oh, so you're a prophet! Well, tell me this: Our ancestors worshiped God at this mountain, but you Jews insist that Jerusalem is the only place to worship, right?" [21-23] "Believe me, woman, the time is coming when you Samaritans will worship the Father neither here at this mountain nor there in Jerusalem. You worship guessing in the dark; we Jews worship in the clear light of day. God's way off salvation is made available through the Jews. But the time is coming – it has, in fact, come – when what you're called will not matter and where you go to worship will not matter. [23-24] "It's who you are and the way you live that count before God. Your worship must engage your spirit in the pursuit of truth. That's the kind of people the Father is out looking for: those who are simply and honestly* ***themselves*** *before him in their worship. God is sheer being itself – Spirit. Those who worship him must do it out of their very being, their spirits, their true selves, in adoration." [25] The woman said, "I don't know about that. I do know that the Messiah is coming. When he arrives, we'll get the whole story." [26] "I am he," said Jesus. "You don't have to wait any longer or look any further."*

Well, so much for short and sweet verses! This favorite passage is long (in case you missed that fact), but I'm serious, there was no way to cut it down. Jesus (God) shows up in unexpected places. Pray to realize, acknowledge, and accept His gifts when you receive them.

May 20

**Luke 24:1-3, 39** (NIV) [1] *On the first day of the week, very early in the morning, the women took the spices they had prepared and went to the tomb.* [2] *They found the stone rolled away from the tomb,* [3] *but when they entered, they did not find the body of the Lord Jesus.* [39] *[*Jesus said] "Look at my hands and my feet. It is I myself! Touch me and see; a ghost does not have flesh and bones, as you see I have."*

One of my very favorite verses because everything changed that morning with the word "but" in verse 3. "He is not here, He is risen!" (see Matthew 28:6) Later in the passage, He appears to two men walking to Emmaus, and they don't recognize Him until He says the blessing over their meal. And later He appears to them again as they are sharing their experience with the 11 apostles. In verse 39, He says, "touch me…a ghost does not have flesh and bones." Those nail-scarred hands are still bringing healing to all who will receive today, just as they did over 2,000 years ago. God allows "do-overs" and U-turns. All we have to do is accept His forgiveness and grace.

*[*My interjection.]*

May 21

**1 Samuel 1:20-28** (MSG) [20]*Before the year was out, Hannah had conceived and given birth to a son. She named him Samuel, explaining, "I asked GOD for him."* [21-22]*When Elkanah next took his family on their annual trip to Shiloh to worship GOD, offering sacrifices and keeping his vow, Hannah didn't go. She told her husband, "After the child is weaned, I'll bring him myself and present him before GOD—and that's where he'll stay, for good."* [23-24]*Elkanah said to his wife, "Do what you think is best. Stay home until you have weaned him. Yes! Let GOD complete what he has begun!" So she did. She stayed home and nursed her son until she had weaned him. Then she took him up to Shiloh, bringing also the makings of a generous sacrificial meal—a prize bull, flour, and wine. The child was so young to be sent off!* [25-28]*They first butchered the bull, then brought the child to Eli. Hannah said, "Excuse me, sir. Would you believe that I'm the very woman who was standing before you at this very spot, praying to GOD? I prayed for this child, and GOD gave me what I asked for. And now I have dedicated him to GOD. He's dedicated to GOD for life." Then and there, they worshiped GOD.*

Be sure and read this whole chapter. It is a favorite passage because Hannah prayed to God as if speaking with a friend. Her example is one we should all follow. He IS our Friend, and He cares about our anguish – no matter what the cause. Pour your heart out to the Lord, as you would to a friend, because God is our Friend. He will hear, answer, and guide you.

May 22

**Hosea 1:2-3** (NIV) [2]*When the LORD began to speak through Hosea, the LORD said to him, "Go, marry a promiscuous woman and have children with her, for like an adulterous wife this land is guilty of unfaithfulness to the LORD."* [3]*So he married Gomer daughter of Diblaim, and she conceived and bore him a son.*

**Hosea 3:1-3** (NIV) [1]*The LORD said to me, "Go, show your love to your wife again, though she is loved by another man and is an adulteress. Love her as the LORD loves the Israelites, though they turn to other gods and love the sacred raisin cakes."* [2]*So I bought her for fifteen shekels of silver and about a homer and a lethek of barley.* [3]*Then I told her, "You are to live with me many days; you must not be a prostitute or be intimate with any man, and I will behave the same way toward you."*

These favorite passages were entered into my journal March 31, 2011. While some may be shocked at this story in the Bible, the love story of Hosea and his prostitute wife mirrors the love story between God and Israel, and between Jesus and His Bride, the Church. This is one of those accounts that totally jumped out and grabbed me. Even though I'd read the Bible through a couple of times, these truths never sank in before that day in March. I encourage y'all to read the entire book of Hosea. It will change your life. Always be open to God's message – the Truth is there!

May 23

**<u>Ephesians 2:8-10</u>** (NIV) [8] *For it is by grace you have been saved, through faith—and this is not from yourselves, it is the gift of God—* [9] *not by works, so that no one can boast.* [10] *For we are God's handiwork, created in Christ Jesus to do good works, which God prepared in advance for us to do.*

Grace and faith can't be earned. Aren't you glad? I know I could NEVER earn what God has given me through Christ. God gives us grace, and we have to make the decision to have faith – exercising the notion that we believe in things we can't see but have the amazing grace [from God] to find the hope we need to believe and move forward. "God's handiwork" is reference to us, the human race. In Verse 10 tells me we are His masterpiece! Enjoy changing – both yourself and others, as a result of the life you choose to lead. God can use us anytime, even when we are scared and unsure – this favorite passage says so!

May 24

**Psalm 107:8** (NIV) *Let them give thanks to the LORD for his unfailing love and his wonderful deeds for mankind.*

So many times, we feel inadequate and less than what we should be – the truth is WE ARE. It is God and God alone Who works in and through us to enable us to do/be what we need to do and to be. This favorite verse reminds us to give thanks for His Mercy, His Strength, and His Love. All of those empower us as we live our lives in Him. As I wrote these words in April 2011, I also wrote the following: **So many thoughts and concerns running through my head – how can I pray for all of them? And then I realized Jesus is the Intercessor and takes the jumbled mess of words and makes them sensible.** Perhaps those words on my heart those many years ago will speak to you today. Even when we don't know how to pray, what to say – just "Father" works.

May 25

**<u>Genesis 1:26-27</u>** (NIV) [26]*Then God said, "Let us make mankind in our image, in our likeness, so that they may rule over the fish in the sea and the birds in the sky, over the livestock and all the wild animals, and over all the creatures that move along the ground."* [27]*So God created mankind in his own image, in the image of God he created them; male and female he created them.*

**<u>Romans 8:6</u>** (NIV) [6] *The mind governed by the flesh is death, but the mind governed by the Spirit is life and peace.*

These two favorite passages remind us we're in the image of God, and that His Spirit needs to govern us. God gave us free will. He gave us a mind to make decisions. We are not robots or puppets. We are uniquely and wonderfully made. Living in the Spirit brings joy and peace. Living in the flesh brings pain and anguish. God wants us to want Him. He wants us to make the decision to accept His gift(s).

May 26

**<u>Mark 10:46-52</u>** (MSG) [46-48]*They spent some time in Jericho. As Jesus was leaving town, trailed by his disciples and a parade of people, a blind beggar by the name of Bartimaeus, son of Timaeus, was sitting alongside the road. When he heard that Jesus the Nazarene was passing by, he began to cry out, "Son of David, Jesus! Mercy, have mercy on me!" Many tried to hush him up, but he yelled all the louder, "Son of David! Mercy, have mercy on me!"* [49-50]*Jesus stopped in his tracks. "Call him over." They called him. "It's your lucky day! Get up! He's calling you to come!" Throwing off his coat, he was on his feet at once and came to Jesus.* [51]*Jesus said, "What can I do for you?" The blind man said, "Rabbi, I want to see."* [52]*"On your way," said Jesus. "Your faith has saved and healed you." In that very instant he recovered his sight and followed Jesus down the road.*

A former pastor, Dr. Tom Davis, preached from this passage and told us to "widen the camera lens and see not only Jesus but also Bartimaeus, who took time to listen and know Jesus was coming." On that day, this passage became a favorite. Jesus took advantage of the interruption. We should also take advantage of the interruptions that come our way, because they can be a *God thing*. Bartimaeus took advantage of heartache to learn. The lesson to us is, even in heartache, we can learn if we spend those times with God.

May 27

**<u>Job 8:20-22</u>** (NIV) [20]*"Surely God does not reject one who is blameless or strengthen the hands of evildoers.* [21] *He will yet fill your mouth with laughter and your lips with shouts of joy.* [22] *Your enemies will be clothed in shame, and the tents of the wicked will be no more."*

God has given us the gift of laughter. It is good for the stomach and it is good for "what ails us". The first time this passage appeared in my journals was April 2011, and it became a favorite. That was 18 months before the worst six months of my life. In October 2012 my sister Gail was murdered. In January 2013 my daddy died. In April 2013, my three-year-old great-nephew, Griffin, drowned. Our family survived those tragedies with our faith and our humor, without which none of us would be standing today.

May 28

**<u>Mark 14:1-9</u>** (MSG) [1-2]*In only two days the eight-day Festival of Passover and the Feast of Unleavened Bread would begin. The high priests and religion scholars were looking for a way they could seize Jesus by stealth and kill him. They agreed that it should not be done during Passover Week. "We don't want the crowds up in arms," they said.* [3-5]*Jesus was at Bethany, a guest of Simon the Leper. While he was eating dinner, a woman came up carrying a bottle of very expensive perfume. Opening the bottle, she poured it on his head. Some of the guests became furious among themselves. "That's criminal! A sheer waste! This perfume could have been sold for well over a year's wages and handed out to the poor." They swelled up in anger, nearly bursting with indignation over her.* [6-9]*But Jesus said, "Let her alone. Why are you giving her a hard time? She has just done something wonderfully significant for me. You will have the poor with you every day for the rest of your lives. Whenever you feel like it, you can do something for them. Not so with me. She did what she could when she could—she pre-anointed my body for burial. And you can be sure that wherever in the whole world the Message is preached, what she just did is going to be talked about admiringly."*

Has anyone ever called you wasteful? Made fun of something you chose to do that was "off the beaten path"? It's happened to me a lot because I'm weird and quirky. My heart and mind march to their own drummer, and occasionally the song I hear isn't the one everyone else is marching to. That's why this passage resonates with me and became a favorite. The woman broke the jar of perfume just as we must break our old attitudes, break open extravagant love, break out with a healing touch. A pat on the back, or a touch on the arm may be just what someone you encounter needs. Follow your heart where God leads you, even if people don't approve. Do something unexpected for God!

May 29

**Matthew 5:14** (NIV) [14] *"You are the light of the world. A town built on a hill cannot be hidden."*

**Isaiah 49:16** (NIV) [16] *See, I have engraved you on the palms of my hands; your walls are ever before me.*

Jesus tells us in Matthew 5:14 that we are the light of the world. We are engraved on His hands. We are to live so all know we are God's. We are to dance to His song of life. How can these not be favorite verses? Through God we are beacons of light to a sick and dying world. Let them see us laugh and love and dance. Worshipping our God and living out His plans for us.

May 30

**Isaiah 30:21** (NIV) *Whether you turn to the right or to the left, your ears will hear a voice behind you, saying, "This is the way; walk in it."*

Holy moly, this favorite verse grabs my soul! One of my favorite contemporary Christian songs is *Voice of Truth*. The lyrics encourage us to listen to God, and not the people in our lives who don't necessarily tell us the truth. God's Word is the Truth, and this passage clearly indicates He is there whispering to us wherever we go. Isn't that the coolest thing ever? Come on y'all, can I get an amen?

May 31

**<u>Psalm 112:7</u>** (NLT) *They do not fear bad news; they confidently trust the LORD to care for them.*

The older I get, the more the meaning of this favorite verse burns in my heart. God is with us always. Remember to go to Him for all things and seek His will, advice, and comfort. There are many times in life that we are knocked about as if we were small trees bending in a hurricane or buckling under the heavy snow of winter. Yet, we stand because God is ALWAYS there! I was blessed beyond measure when God brought my husband, Matthew, into my life. May 31st is special to me because it's his birthday. The two of us have learned to bend and twist together in the storms of life, only to bounce back after the storm clouds pass. That's God, y'all.

June 1

**Daniel 1:8-16** (MSG) *[8-10]But Daniel determined that he would not defile himself by eating the king's food or drinking his wine, so he asked the head of the palace staff to exempt him from the royal diet. The head of the palace staff, by God's grace, liked Daniel, but he warned him, "I'm afraid of what my master the king will do. He is the one who assigned this diet and if he sees that you are not as healthy as the rest, he'll have my head!" [11-13]But Daniel appealed to a steward who had been assigned by the head of the palace staff to be in charge of Daniel, Hananiah, Mishael, and Azariah: "Try us out for ten days on a simple diet of vegetables and water. Then compare us with the young men who eat from the royal menu. Make your decision on the basis of what you see." [14-16]The steward agreed to do it and fed them vegetables and water for ten days. At the end of the ten days they looked better and more robust than all the others who had been eating from the royal menu. So the steward continued to exempt them from the royal menu of food and drink and served them only vegetables.*

To understand the entire story, you may want to read the entire chapter. Basically, the Jews had been taken captive and the young men were going to be made to eat the "king's food" which was unclean for them to eat. Daniel and his three friends decided NOT to eat the unclean food. Daniel was brave enough to speak up, and request that the four of them be allowed to eat what God wanted them to eat. Apparently, they were the only four captives who stood up for what they believed to be right. This is a favorite passage because it reminds me to stand up for my beliefs and principles, even when they are in contrast with the majority. When God places something in hearts that we should do (or NOT do), we should follow His guidance and have faith He will be with us and prepare the way for whatever His plan is. And, if it means having a conversation as Daniel did, do it respectfully, as Daniel did.

June 2

**2 Corinthians 12:9-10** (NIV) [9] *But he said to me, "My grace is sufficient for you, for my power is made perfect in weakness." Therefore I will boast all the more gladly about my weaknesses, so that Christ's power may rest on me.* [10] *That is why, for Christ's sake, I delight in weaknesses, in insults, in hardships, in persecutions, in difficulties. For when I am weak, then I am strong.*

His grace IS sufficient, and in our weakness, we ARE made strong through Him. God did not take away Paul's "thorn" but rather comforted him in the knowledge that God's grace was all he needed. I don't think it's an oversight that we never know what the "thorn" was because not knowing allows us to apply it to anything that may be our own "thorn". I'm comforted in this favorite passage, to know that no matter what I face, God is enough. Hope y'all picked up on that theme… Just checkin'.

June 3

**John 15:13-15** (NIV) [13] *Greater love has no one than this: to lay down one's life for one's friends.* [14] *You are my friends if you do what I command.* [15] *I no longer call you servants, because a servant does not know his master's business. Instead, I have called you friends, for everything that I learned from my Father I have made known to you.*

These are Jesus' words. Through Him, we know everything we need to know about God, just as we share with our friends about our parents and our lives. The fact that He calls us "friends" is such a wonderful blessing! Do y'all see why this is a favorite passage? He loved us enough to lay down His life for us. The key is LOVE and the theme is LIFE. God is LOVE. He gives us LIFE. Jesus LOVED us and gave His LIFE for us. We are His friends! Amen and amen.

June 4

**Isaiah 61:10** (NIV) *I delight greatly in the* L*ORD; my soul rejoices in my God. For he has clothed me with garments of salvation and arrayed me in a robe of his righteousness, as a bridegroom adorns his head like a priest, and as a bride adorns herself with her jewels.*

I delight greatly in this favorite verse because it tells me Jesus approves of us. He doesn't want us motivated by guilt. Can I get an amen?! He wants us to **relax in his perfect love**. He wants us to delight and rejoice in Him. As we reflect on all God has given us, and has done for us, it isn't hard to delight and rejoice in Him. Our being close to God makes Him happy, as well as making us happy. The garments of salvation He gives us are like a bridegroom would give his bride, bringing to mind the special and close relationship God wants with us. Can I get an amen?

June 5

**<u>2 Corinthians 13:3-6</u>** (NLT) [3] *I will give you all the proof you want that Christ speaks through me. Christ is not weak when he deals with you; he is powerful among you.* [4] *Although he was crucified in weakness, he now lives by the power of God. We, too, are weak, just as Christ was, but when we deal with you we will be alive with him and will have God's power.* [5] *Examine yourselves to see if your faith is genuine. Test yourselves. Surely you know that Jesus Christ is among you; if not, you have failed the test of genuine faith.* [6] *As you test yourselves, I hope you will recognize that we have not failed the test of apostolic authority.*

Apparently, some in the congregation of Corinth had been questioning the authority of Paul. Sounds like it could be any church today, right? This is a favorite passage because it speaks of the weakness of Christ. I don't know about you, but I rarely (never) think in terms of His weakness. However, He became weak for us! He allowed Himself to be broken for us. His Power broke the chains of death and weakness when He arose!! Paul had two messages to the church in the verses above: 1) to test their own faith to ensure it was genuine; 2) God's power trumps our weakness. It's always wise to test what we're about to do/say against our faith. And praise be to God His Power trumps my weakness, because when I am weak, HE IS STRONG!

June 6

**Genesis 3:8** (NIV) *Then the man and his wife heard the sound of the LORD God as he was walking in the garden in the cool of the day, and they hid from the LORD God among the trees of the garden.*

**Psalm 89:15** (NIV) *Blessed are those who have learned to acclaim you, who walk in the light of your presence, LORD.*

Living in Christ sets us apart to be in His Presence, to walk with Him. The two favorite verses above give totally opposite scenarios for daily contact with God. Adam and Eve hid due to their disobedience; the Psalmist states how blessed the person who walks in the light of God's presence is. I cannot imagine my life without God walking with me daily through the good, the bad, and the ugly. I don't recall ever wanting to hide from God, but there have been times when I didn't feel His presence. It felt like my prayers were just bouncing off the ceiling. What I came to understand was that I WAS THE ONE WHO LEFT, not God! In the summer and fall of 2009, I began to recognize God's Presence and Peace in a way that I had earlier just taken for granted. I began to realize I, at times, let toxic people/situations affect my journey. God helped me to understand how to recognize when that happens. Ultimately, I learned to free myself of those types of people and situations.

June 7

**Numbers 6:24-26** (NIV) [24] *"The LORD bless you and keep you;*
[25] *the LORD make his face shine on you and be gracious to you;*
[26] *the LORD turn his face toward you and give you peace."*

These are God's words to Moses regarding blessing the Israelites. It is one of my favorite closing prayers at church. It's been a favorite passage for as long as I can remember. The words are such a comfort to me. The visualization of God turning His face toward me DOES give me peace. A peace that passes all understanding. His shining Light on me keeps me on the path of His Light. Oh, man, chill-bump time for me.

June 8

**2 Peter 1:3-9** (NLT) [3]*By his divine power, God has given us everything we need for living a godly life. We have received all of this by coming to know him, the one who called us to himself by means of his marvelous glory and excellence.* [4]*And because of his glory and excellence, he has given us great and precious promises. These are the promises that enable you to share his divine nature and escape the world's corruption caused by human desires.* [5]*In view of all this, make every effort to respond to God's promises. Supplement your faith with a generous provision of moral excellence, and moral excellence with knowledge,* [6]*and knowledge with self-control, and self-control with patient endurance, and patient endurance with godliness,* [7]*and godliness with brotherly affection, and brotherly affection with love for everyone.* [8]*The more you grow like this, the more productive and useful you will be in your knowledge of our Lord Jesus Christ.* [9]*But those who fail to develop in this way are shortsighted or blind, forgetting that they have been cleansed from their old sins.*

This favorite passage is a reminder to continually grow in our faith and to ensure we have the character of Christ. Goodness, knowledge, self-control, perseverance, godliness, brotherly kindness, and love are just a few of the qualities that help us in our efforts to be like Christ. I really like the way the NIV reads that without these characteristics we are ineffective because we are **nearsighted and blind**. A perfect description to me because without my glasses to correct my vision, I wouldn't see clearly. Without the lens of Christ in my Spiritual life, I wouldn't see clearly, either.

June 9

**Isaiah 43:19** (NIV) *See, I am doing a new thing! Now it springs up; do you not perceive it? I am making a way in the wilderness and streams in the wasteland.*

These are the words of God to Isaiah. Sometimes as life happens, we just need to reboot and to KNOW God is with us. He has overcome the world and He will be with us as we overcome life's curve balls. This favorite verse is God's message to me that He's on it and He's engaged in all the aspects of my life, no matter what the wildernesses or the wastelands hold. Can I get an amen?

June 10

**1 Corinthians 16:13** (NIV) *Be on your guard; stand firm in the faith; be courageous; be strong.*

This favorite verse was in my journal dated October 4, 2011, the 52nd anniversary of my walking the aisle of Log Cabin Baptist Church in Macon, GA, to make my public profession of faith. On that day in 1959, I was six years old. Did I totally understand all I needed to know about God? Of course not! I don't totally understand now, and as of this writing I'm 68 years old. It's all about faith in God. Being on our guard, standing firm in our faith, being courageous and strong, and growing in the love and knowledge of our Lord. It's so simple, and yet we make it so hard…

June 11

**Deuteronomy 28:11-14** (NIV) [11]*The LORD will grant you abundant prosperity—in the fruit of your womb, the young of your livestock and the crops of your ground—in the land he swore to your ancestors to give you.* [12]*The LORD will open the heavens, the storehouse of his bounty, to send rain on your land in season and to bless all the work of your hands. You will lend to many nations but will borrow from none.* [13]*The LORD will make you the head, not the tail. If you pay attention to the commands of the LORD your God that I give you this day and carefully follow them, you will always be at the top, never at the bottom.* [14] *Do not turn aside from any of the commands I give you today, to the right or to the left, following other gods and serving them.*

The above favorite passage speaks out in clear and simple terms how to be successful. It was originally written for Israel as they were in the wilderness; however, it would behoove the USA and other nations to adhere to the message in the here and now. God has given us all the directions we need. It's like putting something together: reading the directions is key to getting it right. Trust me on this: just looking at the picture of the finished product, doesn't ensure that you'll put it together properly. You have to READ the instructions! My ADHD brain has trouble with that, but thankfully God's Word is simple enough for a child to understand.

June 12

**<u>Zechariah 4:6-7</u>** (NIV) [6]*So he said to me, "This is the word of the LORD to Zerubbabel: 'Not by might nor by power, but by my Spirit,' says the LORD Almighty.* [7]*"What are you, mighty mountain? Before Zerubbabel you will become level ground. Then he will bring out the capstone to shouts of 'God bless it! God bless it!'"*

You might be wondering why in the world this is a favorite verse. It's because God is willing and able to unleash His power on our behalf. Isn't that cool!? The "mountain" in our lives is no comparison for the mighty Power and Presence of our Lord. Praise God He is with us over, under, around and through the mountains of our lives. Can I get a witness?

June 13

**Matthew 16:13-17** (NIV) [13]*When Jesus came to the region of Caesarea Philippi, he asked his disciples, "Who do people say the Son of Man is?"* [14]*They replied, "Some say John the Baptist; others say Elijah; and still others, Jeremiah or one of the prophets."* [15]*"But what about you?" he asked. "Who do you say I am?"* [16]*Simon Peter answered, "You are the Messiah, the Son of the living God."* [17]*Jesus replied, "Blessed are you, Simon son of Jonah, for this was not revealed to you by flesh and blood, but by my Father in heaven."*

This favorite passage took on an even deeper meaning to me when Matthew and I visited this very place in March 2019. Since that pilgrimage, Scriptures are more vivid because we walked where Jesus walked. Jesus asked the apostles who people said He was. Their answers were: "John the Baptist, Elijah, Jeremiah, or one of the prophets." Then He said, "But what about YOU? Who do you say that I am?" And Peter with his bold personality answered, "You are the Messiah, the Son of the living God." Jesus praised his answer as being revealed by God. It is comforting to me to know that even with the mistakes that Peter made, he was a man of God, just as I am a woman of God in spite of myself.

June 14

**<u>Genesis 2:7</u>** (NIV) *Then the* L*ORD God formed a man from the dust of the ground and breathed into his nostrils the breath of life, and the man became a living being.*

This is such a beautiful verse to me, and easily a favorite. The thought of God breathing life into mankind just gives me chills. And I'll be honest; I don't get caught up in the argument of creation. I don't care "how, when, etc." I care that regardless of the "how, when, etc.", God did it! If that makes me simple, so be it. I like simple. We are to walk with God. We are to have a relationship with Him. We are to feast on His Word.

June 15

**Job 1:20-21** (NIV) [20]*At this, Job got up and tore his robe and shaved his head. Then he fell to the ground in worship* [21]*and said: "Naked I came from my mother's womb, and naked I will depart. The Lord gave and the LORD has taken away; may the name of the LORD be praised."*

Job had great faith in the face of losing all he had. This favorite passage emphasizes what's truly important in life. Job recognized that all he had was of God. Allowing God into our lives lets him shine light in our darkness and give us strength in our weakness. Without God we are nothing. Knowing Jesus is with me makes my life bearable always - even in the darkest days; even when I feel I can't put one foot in front of the other. I came into this world with nothing, and I'll leave this world with nothing. In between those two times – God, always, GOD.

June 16

**<u>Matthew 8:5-13</u>** (NLT) [5]*When Jesus returned to Capernaum, a Roman officer came and pleaded with him,* [6]*"Lord, my young servant lies in bed, paralyzed and in terrible pain."* [7]*Jesus said, "I will come and heal him."* [8]*But the officer said, "Lord, I am not worthy to have you come into my home. Just say the word from where you are, and my servant will be healed.* [9]*I know this because I am under the authority of my superior officers, and I have authority over my soldiers. I only need to say, 'Go,' and they go, or 'Come,' and they come. And if I say to my slaves, 'Do this,' they do it."* [10]*When Jesus heard this, he was amazed. Turning to those who were following him, he said, "I tell you the truth, I haven't seen faith like this in all Israel!* [11]*And I tell you this, that many Gentiles will come from all over the world—from east and west—and sit down with Abraham, Isaac, and Jacob at the feast in the Kingdom of Heaven.* [12]*But many Israelites—those for whom the Kingdom was prepared—will be thrown into outer darkness, where there will be weeping and gnashing of teeth."* [13]*Then Jesus said to the Roman officer, "Go back home. Because you believed, it has happened." And the young servant was healed that same hour.*

This favorite passage points out that people are watching us. They know who and Whose we are by our actions. I pray my actions reflect God. Jesus sent us out to change the world by learning how to live by faith and sharing that faith with others. The centurion had been watching Jesus and believed His Power. We, too, can watch Jesus and believe His power. We who know Him are to live like we are His children so others will believe as well.

June 17

**Hebrews 11:1-2** (NIV) [1]*Now faith is confidence in what we hope for and assurance about what we do not see.* [2] *This is what the ancients were commended for.*

I love these verses, and that makes them favorites. Their meaning is the essence of my belief system. No, I can't see all the things I KNOW about God; but I know them because of my confidence in Him and His Word. I BELIEVE just as our forefathers in faith believed. That's what faith is. Again, may be simple, but simple works for me.

June 18

**<u>Daniel 3:16-18</u>** (NIV) [16] *Shadrach, Meshach and Abednego replied to him, "King Nebuchadnezzar, we do not need to defend ourselves before you in this matter.* [17] *If we are thrown into the blazing furnace, the God we serve is able to deliver us from it, and he will deliver us from Your Majesty's hand.* [18] *But even if he does not, we want you to know, Your Majesty, that we will not serve your gods or worship the image of gold you have set up."*

Even though I've read these verses many times, they became favorites when it finally jumped out to me that they told the king they knew God could deliver them, but "even if He does not", they wouldn't serve his false gods. What an amazingly faithful statement to make! This resonates with me because I attended a funeral where the young mother who died had written an open letter primarily to her two pre-teen daughters, but also to those of us attending the funeral. She wrote in the letter how she'd prayed for healing, "but even if He didn't" she would always serve Him. Her faith never faltered throughout the two years she battled cancer. Her life was a witness to all of us. "Even if He does not", God is!

June 19

**Romans 5:1-5** (NIV) [1]*Therefore, since we have been justified through faith, we have peace with God through our Lord Jesus Christ* [2]*through whom we have gained access by faith into this grace in which we now stand. And we boast in the hope of the glory of God.* [3]*Not only so, but we also glory in our sufferings, because we know that suffering produces perseverance;* [4]*perseverance, character; and character, hope.* [5]*And hope does not put us to shame, because God's love has been poured out into our hearts through the Holy Spirit, who has been given to us.*

This favorite passage has always spoken to me. Realizing the value of the "valley" experiences helped me understand they were producing in me the perseverance, character and hope that I would need to get THROUGH them. Also, realizing that God escorts me through the "valley" experiences has given me the ability to walk through the rough times, or allow Him to carry me, as the case may be.

June 20

**1 Thessalonians 1:1-7** (NLT) *[1]This letter is from Paul, Silas, and Timothy. We are writing to the church in Thessalonica, to you who belong to God the Father and the Lord Jesus Christ. May God give you grace and peace. [2]We always thank God for all of you and pray for you constantly. [3]As we pray to our God and Father about you, we think of your faithful work, your loving deeds, and the enduring hope you have because of our Lord Jesus Christ. [4]We know, dear brothers and sisters, that God loves you and has chosen you to be his own people. [5]For when we brought you the Good News, it was not only with words but also with power, for the Holy Spirit gave you full assurance that what we said was true. And you know of our concern for you from the way we lived when we were with you. [6]So you received the message with joy from the Holy Spirit in spite of the severe suffering it brought you. In this way, you imitated both us and the Lord. [7]As a result, you have become an example to all the believers in Greece—throughout both Macedonia and Achaia.*

These first seven verses of 1 Thessalonians are favorites because they set the stage for the two books that have so much information to help us live as we should. Paul is commending the church at Thessalonica for their growth in Christ and how their lives ring out the message of Christ. Both books of Thessalonians show us how to live out our faith. We are to be proactive vs. reactive. Regardless of the circumstances Satan may throw our way, God is God and HE is always with us in life's ups and downs. We are to pray for each other continually.

June 21

**Micah 6:8** (NIV) *He has shown you, O mortal, what is good. And what does the* L*ORD* *require of you? To act justly and to love mercy and to walk humbly with your God.*

The thought of walking with God brings me peace. We are the ultimate creation of God. We are to act justly and love mercy. Walking with Him allows us to commune with Him and learn His ways. This favorite verse reminds me of John Wesley's *Three Simple Rules*: *Do good; Do no harm; Stay in love with God.* That sums it up in a nutshell, y'all. Can't get any clearer than that.

June 22

**Romans 12:2** (NIV) *Do not conform to the pattern of this world, but be transformed by the renewing of your mind. Then you will be able to test and approve what God's will is—his good, pleasing and perfect will.*

No matter how busy I am – whether projects at home, projects helping others, or writing/preparing presentations, or even writing a devotional book – I need to STOP and spend quality time with my God. This favorite verse reminds me of my need to renew my mind and my heart, and my soul. The world promotes a rat race that gets us nowhere, except perhaps in the doctor's office due to stress. Our souls need and crave quality time with God, Who renews and refreshes us.

June 23

**<u>Philippians 4:7</u>** (NIV) *And the peace of God, which transcends all understanding, will guard your hearts and your minds in Christ Jesus.*

When I initially entered this verse into my journal, I was using a devotional book with many verses each day. During that period in my life our mom, who had been caring for our dad (Alzheimer's patient) at home, had fallen and broken her hip. Our family had to make the gut-wrenching decision to place Daddy in a facility. This verse spoke to me that morning, and I KNOW beyond any shadow of a doubt that God led me to this favorite verse.

June 24

**Joshua 1:2, 5, 9** (NIV) [2] *"Moses my servant is dead. Now then, you and all these people, get ready to cross the Jordan River into the land I am about to give to them—to the Israelites. [5] No one will be able to stand against you all the days of your life. As I was with Moses, so I will be with you; I will never leave you nor forsake you. [9] Have I not commanded you? Be strong and courageous. Do not be afraid; do not be discouraged, for the LORD your God will be with you wherever you go."*

This is God talking to Joshua. The Israelites are about to enter the Promised Land about 600 years after the original promise to Abraham. This favorite passage teaches us that when God promises us something, He means it and He will do what He says! Not only is He fulfilling His promise to Abraham, He is making a promise to Joshua to be with him. He makes that same promise to us today. So many times, when I have an issue with someone, I find myself rehearsing our conversation. How ridiculous is that when I can't possibly know what he/she is thinking or what will be said. Instead of rehearsing, my energy is best spent praying for the response God would have me say. Can I get an amen?

June 25

**<u>Ephesians 1:18-20</u>** (NIV) [18] *I pray that the eyes of your heart may be enlightened in order that you may know the hope to which he has called you, the riches of his glorious inheritance in his holy people,* [19] *and his incomparably great power for us who believe. That power is the same as the mighty strength* [20] *he exerted when he raised Christ from the dead and seated him at his right hand in the heavenly realms.*

This is Paul writing to the church at Ephesus, reminding them to turn the eyes of their hearts on God. It is as pertinent today as the day it was written and spoken to the people back then. Grasping the implications of our relationship with God; and embracing His love, power, and strength, makes all the difference in our journey. And our journey may make all the difference in someone else's life. This favorite passage ensures I don't forget that.

June 26

**<u>Romans 6:3-4, 20-23</u>** (CSB) *[3] Or are you unaware that all of us who were baptized into Christ Jesus were baptized into his death? [4] Therefore we were buried with him by baptism into death, in order that, just as Christ was raised from the dead by the glory of the Father, so we too may walk in newness of life. [20] For when you were slaves of sin, you were free with regard to righteousness. [21] So what fruit was produced then from the things you are now ashamed of? The outcome of those things is death. [22] But now, since you have been set free from sin and have become enslaved to God, you have your fruit, which results in sanctification—and the outcome is eternal life! [23] For the wages of sin is death, but the gift of God is eternal life in Christ Jesus our Lord.*

This favorite passage always breeds great discussion – falling from grace; becoming "unsaved"; etc. My personal belief is that one's salvation remains intact, regardless of your choices. As one pastor put it, that's ETERNAL SECURITY. However, the quality of your walk, the closeness of your relationship with God, and your witness to others is most definitely affected, and many times marred, by inappropriate behavior. Eternal security does not erase the consequences of our choices.

June 27

**Isaiah 2:5; 60:2** **(NIV)** [5]*Come, descendants of Jacob, let us walk in the light of the LORD.* [2]*See, darkness covers the earth and thick darkness is over the peoples, but the LORD rises upon you and his glory appears over you.*

We are reflections to the world of the love and light of God. We should choose our words carefully, monitor our actions and reactions in such a way that God's love and light flows through us and out to the world. These favorite verses first appeared in my journal one December day a few years ago. How appropriate, I thought, as it was my sister, Kathy's, birthday. Her life is an example to all of us how it IS possible to be God's light and love.

June 28

**Mark 10:13-16:** **(NIV)** [13] *People were bringing little children to Jesus for him to place his hands on them, but the disciples rebuked them.* [14] *When Jesus saw this, he was indignant. He said to them, "Let the little children come to me, and do not hinder them, for the kingdom of God belongs to such as these.* [15] *Truly I tell you, anyone who will not receive the kingdom of God like a little child will never enter it."* [16] *And he took the children in his arms, placed his hands on them and blessed them.*

It breaks my heart to see some churches not embracing and respecting their children and youth. As Mark writes, it's not a new problem. Quite clearly and sternly, Christ rebuked the disciples who tried to send the children away. Children's faith is beautiful, honest, total, complete trust. Not only should we respect and nurture that, we should also practice it, as this favorite passage reflects.

June 29

**<u>Isaiah 53:3-7</u>** (NIV) [3]*He was despised and rejected by mankind, a man of suffering, and familiar with pain. Like one from whom people hide their faces he was despised, and we held him in low esteem.* [4]*Surely he took up our pain and bore our suffering, yet we considered him punished by God, stricken by him, and afflicted.* [5]*But he was pierced for our transgressions, he was crushed for our iniquities; the punishment that brought us peace was on him, and by his wounds we are healed.* [6]*We all, like sheep, have gone astray, each of us has turned to our own way; and the LORD has laid on him the iniquity of us all.* [7] *He was oppressed and afflicted, yet he did not open his mouth; he was led like a lamb to the slaughter, and as a sheep before its shearers is silent, so he did not open his mouth.*

As I read this favorite passage, it brought back memories of my childhood when I was in GAs (Girls' Auxiliary in the Southern Baptist Church). Verse 6 was our watchword. My heart breaks that many (too many) of our religious leaders of today act toward Christ the way many of them did in His time on earth. They totally seem to miss His message of love, acceptance, and no judgment. That's really a sad commentary since we know "the rest of the story". My prayer is that the church community will embrace God's love and grace, and share His message to all by our actions.

June 30

**James 1:2-4 (NIV)** *[2]Consider it pure joy, my brothers and sisters, whenever you face trials of many kinds, [3]because you know that the testing of your faith produces perseverance. [4]Let perseverance finish its work so that you may be mature and complete, not lacking anything.*

The date of the entry in my journal was October 14, 2012 - eight days after we found out my sister, Gail had been murdered. I wrote: **I am not to a place to consider what has happened pure joy – and maybe Paul didn't mean situations such as the death of a loved one. Maybe he was talking about just day-to-day trials. In all situations God is at work and through Him we become stronger**. Notes in my Bible margins read: **"not simply to suffer but to overcome"**; **"ability to turn things into greatness and glory"**. Today, as I revisit this favorite passage to include in this book, I still have no "joy" regarding Gail's death. I DO, however, have and embrace the joy of my salvation and of my walk with God. He, and ONLY HE, carried me and my family through those horrible days in 2012, as well as each day and moment since that we've lived without the ability to call, see, or be with our Gail.

July 1

**Luke 24: 27-32 (NIV)** [27]*And beginning with Moses and all the Prophets, he explained to them what was said in all the Scriptures concerning himself.* [28]*As they approached the village to which they were going, Jesus continued on as if he were going farther.* [29]*But they urged him strongly, "Stay with us, for it is nearly evening; the day is almost over." So he went in to stay with them.* [30]*When he was at the table with them, he took bread, gave thanks, broke it and began to give it to them.* [31]*Then their eyes were opened and they recognized him, and he disappeared from their sight.* [32]*They asked each other, "Were not our hearts burning within us while he talked with us on the road and opened the Scriptures to us?"*

You may want to start reading at verse 13 and continue through verse 35 for the entire story, but the verses I've chosen hit the gist of this favorite passage. I can only imagine how amazing it would be to see Jesus in the flesh. This first appeared in my journals on December 28, 2011. The previous two months had been a blur to me as we experienced one trauma after another: I had a serious dog bite, Mom broke her hip, it became apparent she could no longer care for Daddy and we had to place him in a memory care facility. None of us realized how serious his Alzheimer's had gotten until then. Life rolled on those two months like a freight train with no brakes. I got caught up in the "fast track" rather than savoring moments I could and giving thanks for the miracles along the way. That's the same thing that happened to the people traveling to Emmaus. Jesus was right there with them and they never stopped to really listen and KNOW it was Him. My prayer is that God will help me keep my eyes and heart open always for His Presence and His miracles. I'm telling y'all, it may not be physically possible at this time to actually be with Jesus, but thanks to the Holy Spirit within us, we are always in His presence. Can I get an amen?

July 2

**<u>Genesis 3:1</u>** (NIV) *Now the serpent was more crafty than any of the wild animals the LORD God had made. He said to the woman, "Did God really say, 'You must not eat from any tree in the garden'?"*

So, this is where it all began. Sin entered into our world via a serpent in the garden God had made because Eve was like all of us, and didn't recognize the evil. That's why this verse is a favorite. It reminds me of the craftiness of Satan, and to be aware of his evil. The apple looked good. Surely God hadn't meant to deprive her and Adam. One little bite won't hurt…. Sounds pretty familiar, right? Evil began then and has been a part of our journey ever since. The GOOD NEWS is that God had a plan then, and He's still carrying out that plan now through Jesus. He helps us combat the evil and gives us the tools we need to survive outside the garden.

July 3

**Job 2:9-10** (NIV) [9] *His wife said to him, "Are you still maintaining your integrity? Curse God and die!"* [10] *He replied, "You are talking like a foolish woman. Shall we accept good from God, and not trouble?" In all this, Job did not sin in what he said.*

I don't believe and won't believe that BAD comes from a loving God. I will also never curse God when bad happens for the same reason. He allows bad, because sin is in the world and humans are not puppets. Free will is available to good and bad people, and unfortunately, some really bad things happen as a result. However, God works everything out to conform to His will - even (maybe especially) the bad things that happen to us. He doesn't cause bad, He takes bad and makes good come of it. This favorite passage reminds me to have my faith anchored in God no matter what. As I write this, our nation is experiencing the COVID-19 pandemic. Many of us are under a "shelter in place" directive. It's one of the worst things our nation has experienced. Even in this, GOD is with us. Amen!

July 4

**2 Chronicles 7:14** (NIV) *if my people, who are called by my name, will humble themselves and pray and seek my face and turn from their wicked ways, then I will hear from heaven, and I will forgive their sin and will heal their land.*

Amen and amen – humble ourselves, pray, and God will heal us. Sounds so simple, and yet many of us have trouble implementing these into our daily lives. Why is that? The answers will be as different as we are from one another, but the solution is One and His name is God, Holy Father, Trinity, Almighty, the great I AM. What better verse than this favorite for the 4$^{th}$ of July.

July 5

**Psalm 31:19-20** (NIV) [19] *How abundant are the good things that you have stored up for those who fear you, that you bestow in the sight of all, on those who take refuge in you.* [20] *In the shelter of your presence you hide them from all human intrigues; you keep them safe in your dwelling from accusing tongues.*

I can rest in God's love. He is with me always and I can "hide" in Him as I've done in His "rocking chair" many times. As silly as it may sound, many a night when I'm fearful and/or wrestling with one of life's curve balls, I visualize myself climbing into the lap of God and Him rocking me like a parent soothes a young child. That's why these verses are favorites – He is my refuge! Viewing all that happens to us through the lens of God's love allows us to embrace His power of comfort and the help and peace He gives us.

July 6

**2 Corinthians 5:7** (NIV) *For we live by faith, not by sight.*

Faith is believing/trusting when you can't fully explain why. You just KNOW in your heart. Hands down, this is a favorite verse and a mantra for me. The Holy Spirit guides us, so we should strive to be in step with the teaching of God as we live out our day-to-day journey. Many times, we can't SEE what He is doing, but we can FEEL His Presence and His Peace. That is living by faith. Knowing that He is there/here no matter what. In keeping myself open to feeling God's Presence, I learn and experience all that He has for me.

July 7

**Habakkuk 3:17-19** (NIV) [17] *Though the fig tree does not bud and there are no grapes on the vines, though the olive crop fails and the fields produce no food, though there are no sheep in the pen and no cattle in the stalls,* [18] *yet I will rejoice in the LORD, I will be joyful in God my Savior.* [19] *The Sovereign LORD is my strength; he makes my feet like the feet of a deer, he enables me to tread on the heights.*

This favorite passage speaks to me because no matter what, God will get us through it. Many stressful, awful events are listed in this passage, and yet the writer tells us "but wait, we have God, our Strength!" These verses speak to me because in the past I had a tendency to go "bonkers" during the hiccups of my day. Learning to lean on God during those times has decreased my stress level, as well as the stress levels of those witnessing my "bonker" moments. The latter part of this verse indicates this is a song; so not only does God give us strength, He gives us a song in our hearts. We can run like a deer and embrace the peace of God! Y'all with me?

July 8

**Jeremiah 29:11** (NIV) *"For I know the plans I have for you," declares the LORD, "plans to prosper you and not to harm you, plans to give you hope and a future."*

This favorite verse tells me that God has a master plan for each of us. Just like the plans we make for ourselves, achieving the goals require action on our part. Staying in-tune with God is vital in carrying out His plans in our lives. Living in God's truth, love, and peace will make us prosperous in the important things of life. The bad days will come for all of us, but holding onto His promises will get us through them, and we will learn from them and grow as we look back and see His handiwork in our lives.

July 9

<u>**Romans 8:18-28**</u> (CSB) *[18]For I consider that the sufferings of this present time are not worth comparing with the glory that is going to be revealed to us. [19]For the creation eagerly waits with anticipation for God's sons to be revealed. [20]For the creation was subjected to futility—not willingly, but because of him who subjected it—in the hope [21]that the creation itself will also be set free from the bondage to decay into the glorious freedom of God's children. [22]For we know that the whole creation has been groaning together with labor pains until now. [23]Not only that, but we ourselves who have the Spirit as the firstfruits—we also groan within ourselves, eagerly waiting for adoption, the redemption of our bodies. [24]Now in this hope we were saved, but hope that is seen is not hope, because who hopes for what he sees? [25]Now if we hope for what we do not see, we eagerly wait for it with patience. [26]In the same way the Spirit also helps us in our weakness, because we do not know what to pray for as we should, but the Spirit himself intercedes for us with inexpressible groanings. [27]And he who searches our hearts knows the mind of the Spirit, because he intercedes for the saints according to the will of God. [28]We know that all things work together for the good of those who love God, who are called according to his purpose.*

This favorite passage paints a picture of my life. Troubles are here because of original sin. Much like a pregnant woman awaits the birth of her child, we await our adoption into the family of God through the redemption that Jesus brought into the world. As children of God, we are heirs with Christ, and we wait patiently on this earth for God to work out the details in His time. While we wait, we hope in Him, allowing our faith to work in us as God prepares our hearts, minds, and souls to be beacons of His love. There are times we don't know how or what to pray. At those times the very Spirit of God intercedes for us. I don't know about you, but that's awesome to me!

July 10

**<u>2 Corinthians 5:</u>17** (NIV) *Therefore, if anyone is in Christ, the new creation has come: The old has gone, the new is here!*

This favorite verse points out that when we are in Christ, our lives are 180° different from when we are NOT in Christ. Old becomes new. Often, we are stuck in the ruts of our circumstances. Many times, we have caused our ruts. Other times, the ruts are beyond our control. However, each day is a new day, and we need to lean on Christ and look at our lives from His perspective. When we do that, our lives - and our ruts - will look different through the Light of His Love.

July 11

**Colossians 3:1-4** (NIV) [1] *Since, then, you have been raised with Christ, set your hearts on things above, where Christ is, seated at the right hand of God.* [2] *Set your minds on things above, not on earthly things.* [3] *For you died, and your life is now hidden with Christ in God.* [4] *When Christ, who is your life, appears, then you also will appear with him in glory.*

This favorite passage reminds me that I died to sin and am now hidden with Christ in God. Of course, this doesn't mean I never sin. My family and friends will attest to that! It means I'm forgiven of my sins, and because of my relationship with Christ I catch myself, and realize what I'm doing isn't right. I wish I could say that the minute I realize I'm wrong I stop doing whatever it is, but alas that would not be true. When I offend someone, I own what I've done, and I confess to them as well as God. I ask forgiveness. This passage also makes me consider that no one is perfect and without sin, and that helps me forgive others.

July 12

**<u>John 21:19b-23</u>** (NIV) [19]*Then he* [*Jesus] *said to him* [*Peter], *"Follow me!"* [20]*Peter turned and saw that the disciple whom Jesus loved* [*John] *was following them. (This was the one who had leaned back against Jesus at the supper and had said, "Lord, who is going to betray you?")* [21]*When Peter saw him, he asked, "Lord, what about him?"* [22]*Jesus answered, "If I want him to remain alive until I return, what is that to you? You must follow me."* [23]*Because of this, the rumor spread among the believers that this disciple would not die. But Jesus did not say that he would not die; he only said, "If I want him to remain alive until I return, what is that to you?"*

Peter was more concerned about John than himself. Isn't that just like us sometimes? We're worried about what someone else is doing, rather than making sure we ourselves are on track. That's why this passage is a favorite. We are to follow God and look to Him for guidance and peace. He has a plan for each person. We are all unique, and God knows that and builds the plan around the uniqueness of individuals. Therefore, we are to base our choices on God, not what others think or do, nor on what we perceive God has done for them and not for us. Very clear admonition from Jesus to mind our own business.

*[* My interjections.]*

July 13

**<u>1 Peter 1:8-9</u>** (NIV) [8] *Though you have not seen him, you love him; and even though you do not see him now, you believe in him and are filled with an inexpressible and glorious joy,*[9] *for you are receiving the end result of your faith, the salvation of your souls.*

Believing and trusting even though we have not SEEN is true faith. That's why I love this passage, and it is a favorite! He fills us with joy so amazing that we can't fully describe it. Communing with Him keeps us filled with His love and joy. It keeps us focused on where He is leading us. It keeps us in tune with His ways. It helps us relate better to others. Without Jesus, my life would be void. No peace. No joy. No love. No happiness. With Jesus my life is complete – unafraid, happy, victorious. Spending time alone with Him is my Source of Strength. Shout to the Lord and worship Him! Can I get an amen?

July 14

**James 1:2-3** (NIV) [2]*Consider it pure joy, my brothers and sisters, whenever you face trials of many kinds,* [3]*because you know that the testing of your faith produces perseverance.*

Perhaps James is speaking specifically to people doing the work of God; but I also believe this favorite passage speaks to the trials we encounter in life. Even though I don't believe God causes the trials to test our faith, I know trials DO test our faith. It is difficult in the midst of pain and suffering to rejoice or even see light at the end of the tunnel. However, we must cling to the fact that no matter what, God is with us. He gives us the ability to overcome and turn things into greatness and glory. In Him we can have pure Joy! The more we overcome, or persevere as it says in verse 3, the easier it is to overcome. The challenges of life are too great to handle without God. He is The Light right there with us. We don't have to wait until the end of the tunnel!

July 15

**<u>Matthew 6:33</u>** (NIV) *But seek first his kingdom and his righteousness, and all these things will be given to you as well.*

This favorite verse is Jesus speaking. It is short, sweet, and to the point: Put God first in your life. This does not mean we won't have problems. It doesn't mean He will make all our issues magically go away, or that we will get everything we want. It means we will find that whatever is going on and whatever path we are on is much easier to navigate when we are focused on God. He truly will hold our hand, guide us, and give us love and peace through it all. I don't know this just because I read the Bible; I know it because it is my life.

July 16

**<u>1 John 4:12</u>** (NIV) *No one has ever seen God; but if we love one another, God lives in us and his love is made complete in us.*

We are to live our lives in such a way that we allow God's love to flow through us and out to a world desperately searching, even though many have no clue what or Whom they are searching for. This favorite verse reminds me to live in such a way that I reflect God. By loving one another, and by reaching out to others with love, we may be the only glimpse of God some people will see.

July 17

**Psalm 18:30** (NIV) *As for God, his way is perfect: The LORD's word is flawless; he shields all who take refuge in him.*

God's way IS perfect. This favorite verse spells it out. Not only is His Way perfect, His Word is flawless – God does NOT lie. We need to trust in Him and not scurry on so far ahead of Him that we turn loose of His hand. He wants to be our shield and our refuge. He won't push Himself on us, we must seek Him through prayer and Bible study. And once we allow God in, He shelters us under His wings like a mother hen shelters her chicks.

July 18

**Hebrews 6:17-20** (NIV) [17] *Because God wanted to make the unchanging nature of His purpose very clear to the heirs of what was promised, he confirmed it with an oath.* [18] *God did this so that, by two unchangeable things in which it is impossible for God to lie, we who have fled to take hold of the hope set before us may be greatly encouraged.* [19] *We have this hope as an anchor for the soul, firm and secure. It enters the inner sanctuary behind the curtain,* [20] *where our forerunner, Jesus, has entered on our behalf. He has become a high priest forever, in the order of Melchizedek**.*

I love the way this favorite passage mentions God's "hope as an anchor for the soul". Growing up in Hanahan, SC (10 miles north of Charleston), I'm all about nautical things. God as my ANCHOR resonates with me. Faith is believing and trusting when you can't fully explain why. You just KNOW in your heart that it is true. We say we believe God, and yet we spend a good bit of time fretting about things. I am so guilty of rehearsing what I'll say in any given situation, rather than just waiting on the Lord and relying on Him to have my back – even including my words! We need to align ourselves with His Word and the "stuff" will fall into place. Rest in the Truth that your Anchor is God, and when your boat is rockin' it won't go far. Amen!

*[*I had to look this up. He was the first individual to be given the title Kohen (priest) in the Hebrew Bible. See Genesis 14:18-20.]*

July 19

**<u>Proverbs 17:22</u>** (NIV) *A cheerful heart is good medicine, but a crushed spirit dries up the bones.*

Out attitude affects our demeanor, and even sometimes our physical well-being. This favorite Proverb says that very clearly. Not only does it affect ALL of our person, it also affects all those around us. We should be mindful of this as we navigate the ups and downs of life. Leading by example is a way of sharing God with our family and friends without being preachy or "holier than thou". Showing, by how we react to life's curve balls, that we KNOW God has our back! Let's live like we believe it. Can I get an amen?

July 20

**<u>Psalm 21:6-7</u>** (NIV) [6] *Surely you have granted him unending blessings and made him glad with the joy of your presence.* [7] *For the king trusts in the* LORD; *through the unfailing love of the Most High he will not be shaken.*

This favorite passage reminds us that God has granted all of us unending blessings. I'm not talking about possessions or wealth. I'm talking about the peace, joy, and contentment our faith brings us. Some of us haven't even realized there were blessings to be had. One must believe, trust, and accept God into their life to receive the blessings. Praise God, just as King David did, I too, walk with God and am blessed and made glad through my relationship with God. I have confidence in God's unfailing love for me. I want all of you to experience this. If you haven't already put your trust in God, I promise you won't regret doing so.

July 21

**Psalm 9:10** (NIV) *Those who know your name trust in you, for you, LORD, have never forsaken those who seek you.*

This favorite verse reminds us that if you know God, you will trust Him. And if you trust Him you will seek Him. He has never forsaken anyone who sought Him. So why do we occasionally feel as if He has? The nagging doubts infiltrate us when we lose sight of Whose we are. We are God's children, and we must keep our eyes and hearts tuned and turned to Him. This verse isn't talking about God knowing us, but He does. He knows us, just like a Shepherd knows his/her sheep. God calls us by our names. As I write this in 2021, this date would have been my best friend, Iris's 69th birthday. Unfortunately, early-onset Alzheimer's took her life way too early. About nine months before she died, I spent the weekend with her. One morning at breakfast she said, "Deb, sometimes I look in the mirror and I don't know my name." I wasn't sure how to respond, and as I was thinking of a proper response, she continued, "but God knows my name". When you are a child of God, even in the last months of your life, even in the last moments of your life, you KNOW Him, and He KNOWS you.

July 22

**John 6:12-13** (NIV) [12] *When they had all had enough to eat, he* [*Jesus] *said to his disciples, "Gather the pieces that are left over. Let nothing be wasted."* [13] *So they gathered them and filled twelve baskets with the pieces of the five barley loaves left over by those who had eaten.*

After the 5,000** had been fed from 5 loaves and 2 fish, 12 baskets of leftovers were gathered! This is a favorite verse because it states clearly that God is more than sufficient to meet our needs – both physical and Spiritual. He is our refuge, light, and life. He never fails us. Rest in Him. I can be confident in life, happy, and unafraid because I walk with God, allowing Him to lead me. He holds my hand and helps me overcome fears. He is unchanging.

*[ * My interjection.]*

*[**Really more people, because only men were counted back in the day.]*

July 23

**1 Peter 3:15** (NIV) *But in your hearts revere Christ as Lord. Always be prepared to give an answer to everyone who asks you to give the reason for the hope that you have. But do this with gentleness and respect.*

I love this favorite verse. We should always be able to tell what Jesus means to us, and why living with Him as our Lord is the ONLY WAY for us. I've never embraced the "cramming the Gospel down your throat" method that some use. This tends to push people away. If you're asked a question about God/faith/Jesus, and you don't know the answer, be honest. Say, "I don't know, but I will search for an answer and get back with you". Living out my faith for others to see, and telling my own story is how I prefer to talk about God. To me, that can draw people to Christ because we are living witnesses.

July 24

**Lamentations 3:22-26** (MSG*)* [22-24]*GOD's loyal love couldn't have run out, his merciful love couldn't have dried up. They're created new every morning. How great your faithfulness! I'm sticking with GOD (I say it over and over). He's all I've got left.* [25-27] *GOD proves to be good to the man who passionately waits, to the woman who diligently seeks. It's a good thing to quietly hope, quietly hope for help from GOD. It's a good thing when you're young to stick it out through the hard times.*

Waiting on God equips us for everything. This favorite passage spells it out beautifully! He will make known the path of life, helping us soar as eagles. When we have Christ, we have ALL we need. We are transformed in Him. He is our first love, He is our Hope of Glory. God's love will NEVER run out. We just have to open our eyes and hearts and focus on Him. As I walked the "long goodbye", as Alzheimer's has been described, with my daddy it was some of the darkest days of my life. Yet I was confident in God to supply my needs, and He did.

July 25

**Isaiah 26:3** (NIV) *You will keep in perfect peace those whose minds are steadfast, because they trust in you.*

This favorite verse reminds me that NOTHING can separate me from the Power of God – except me, when I choose to pull away. The “you” in the above verse is God. Even in the most awful situation imaginable, we have the Peace of God if we trust Him with a child-like faith. Complete and total trust. God will hold us in His hands. True peace comes from God, even in times of chaos. We can’t SEE the wind, but we feel the wind and we see evidence of it. It is the same with God. We feel God and we see the evidence of Him in our lives. No matter what circumstances we find ourselves in, God IS right there with us.

July 26

**Jeremiah 29:13-14** (NIV) [13] *"You will seek me and find me when you seek me with all your heart.* [14] *I will be found by you," declares the* LORD, *"and will bring you back from captivity. I will gather you from all the nations and places where I have banished you," declares the* LORD, *"and will bring you back to the place from which I carried you into exile."*

These favorite verses remind me that when I get into trouble trying to do things on my own, God is still there and all I need is to seek Him. He is easily found. My understanding is just too limited to help me see and know all that is necessary. Trusting the Eternal and Everlasting God is my only hope. God will guide me, protect me from myself as well as my enemies. He will hold me in His arms. He will place me where I need to be.

July 27

**John 20:19** (NIV) *On the evening of that first day of the week, when the disciples were together, with the doors locked for fear of the Jewish leaders, Jesus came and stood among them and said, "Peace be with you!"*

This favorite verse reflects the goodness of God, the fact we can take refuge in Him and find peace. The fact He sees all and knows us for who we are. He IS in the midst of us, regardless of where we are hiding. His Peace changes us. And just like on the day of this passage, He comes in when we're not expecting Him. May we always be aware and feel His Presence in our lives.

July 28

**Zechariah 2:13** (NIV) *Be still before the* L*ORD*, *all mankind, because he has roused himself from his holy dwelling.*

God knows what I need to hear over and over: "Debi, slow down, be still, rest in me." As a result, many of my devotions contain this theme, and here is another favorite verse addressing that. I'm apparently hard-headed and need to be reminded constantly, like a toddler. And even as I wrote this in my journal in April 2012, my phone alarm indicated it was 6:00 a.m. and my daily reminder to "...be still and know that I am God…" scrolled across the face of my phone. Here it is, 2021, and that reminder still scrolls on my phone daily. Amen and amen, Father God, who is with me always and is MY GOD!

July 29

**Isaiah 30:15** (NIV) *This is what the Sovereign LORD, the Holy One of Israel, says: "In repentance and rest is your salvation, in quietness and trust is your strength, but you would have none of it."*

Isaiah was sharing this with Israel, who as a nation had turned their backs on God repeatedly. The message is still true for us today, and I share it as a favorite for that reason. The strength and power we receive from God is real. No matter what our circumstances may be, His Power is in us to sustain us. Spending time with Him in quiet trust, repenting and resting in His everlasting arms gives me the strength to put one foot in front of the other. When we fail to do that our strength is gone. Let it never be said of us, "but you would have none of it".

July 30

**1 John 1:7** (NIV) *But if we walk in the light, as he is in the light, we have fellowship with one another, and the blood of Jesus, his Son, purifies us from all sin.*

We can call on the name of the Lord because Jesus was the ultimate sacrifice. He reconciled us back to God washing away Eve and Adam's sins, as well as our own. Satan is a deceiver and still tries to convince us sin is okay. Sin is NOT okay. We must utter Jesus's name to combat Satan's lies. Only God can purify us. Walking in the Light of Jesus keeps us on the path that He has planned for us, and this favorite verse spells it out clearly. We are washed in His blood.

July 31

**<u>Hebrew 13:8</u>** (NIV) *Jesus Christ is the same yesterday and today and forever.*

Jesus is unchanging. He is solid. He is our anchor. The same: yesterday, today, and forever. I love this favorite verse because with all the winds of life blowing in every direction, it is comforting to know that Jesus is constant. He is consistently Who He presents Himself to be in the Scripture, always and forever. Many things can lend themselves to arguments and disagreements within the interpretation of the Scripture. The fact that Jesus Christ is the same yesterday, today, and forever isn't one of them. Amen and amen.

August 1

**<u>Exodus 33:14</u>** (NIV) *The LORD replied, "My Presence will go with you, and I will give you rest."*

This favorite verse was first entered into my journal on April 9, 2012. I was 59 years old, and I was still learning to lean on God and trust Him and take a leap of faith. I had done so a few weeks earlier, when I resigned from a job my husband and I thought was necessary to survive financially. I knew in my heart God was leading me down a new path, but I'd been afraid to make the leap. During a business call that day in February, I heard God whisper, "you're done," and once I hung up, I called my husband to let him know I was resigning. The peace I felt was incredible. That peace came from God as HE gave me rest. We have NEVER suffered financially as a result of following the whispered voice of God.

August 2

**<u>Philippians 3:13-14</u>** (NIV) [13] *Brothers and sisters, I do not consider myself yet to have taken hold of it. But one thing I do: Forgetting what is behind and straining toward what is ahead,* [14] *I press on toward the goal to win the prize for which God has called me heavenward in Christ Jesus.*

Paul was one of the most real writers of the Bible in that he admitted when he fell short of the mark. His honesty helps me, and I'm sure many other Christians, accept and learn from our mistakes, knowing we have a loving God Who forgives and dusts us off. That's why this passage is a favorite. God picks us up, carries us in some cases, and strengthens us to see the lesson learned, and focus on our eternal goal. Pastor Dr. David Campbell reminded us that "Thy will be done" is NOT prayed from the sidelines. We pray on the field of the Kingdom as we press toward the mark.

August 3

**<u>Exodus 15:22-25a</u>** (NIV) [22] *Then Moses led Israel from the Red Sea and they went into the Desert of Shur. For three days they traveled in the desert without finding water.* [23] *When they came to Marah, they could not drink its water because it was bitter. (That is why the place is called Marah.)* [24] *So the people grumbled against Moses, saying, "What are we to drink?"* [25] *Then Moses cried out to the LORD, and the LORD showed him a piece of wood. He threw it into the water, and the water became fit to drink.*

So many times, we are like the Israelites, "grumble, grumble, grumble". We pick at what isn't perfect, not recognizing the blessings we have from God. I am so guilty of this, and I'm thankful for God's forgiveness. I'm appreciative of this favorite passage which contrasts the grumbling nature of humans and the merciful nature of God. It boils down to trust in ALL circumstances. I realize, finally, what trusting God in/through the bad times means. It means being thankful to God and in tune with God during the bad times, allowing no room for grumbling because our hearts are filled with praise and thanksgiving. Focus on God, not the circumstances.

August 4

**<u>Colossians 3:23</u>** (NIV) *Whatever you do, work at it with all your heart, as working for the Lord, not for human masters.*

As many times as I've read the book of Colossians, for some reason the now-favorite verse above did not jump out and grab me until April 13, 2012. I had no idea that the Bible addressed work ethics spot-on like this verse. Even though I knew as Christians we are to do everything for the Lord, this was a WOW moment for me. The Bible is and always will be relevant! Can I get an amen? God always has and always will be with us as His Word guides our lives.

August 5

__1 Corinthians 15:20-23__ (NIV) [20] *But Christ has indeed been raised from the dead, the firstfruits of those who have fallen asleep.* [21] *For since death came through a man, the resurrection of the dead comes also through a man.* [22] *For as in Adam all die, so in Christ all will be made alive.* [23] *But each in turn: Christ, the firstfruits; then, when he comes, those who belong to him.*

As I began writing this page, I googled “firstfruits” to see if it was one word or two words, since my MAC thought it should be two words. However, I decided to leave it as one word since all references in my Bible were one word. It was then I realized Satan was messing with me to get me off task chasing some spelling rabbit, and not embracing the message of this favorite passage. The point of these verses is that Jesus indeed has risen. He’s broken the chains of death, and as a result all Christians shall rise in Him. I love how it brings up the sin of Adam, which dominoed* us all to sin; then Christ Jesus, Who washed those sins away with His blood.

[*My MAC doesn’t like dominoed either, but it’s my past tense of a bunch of dominoes falling. Work with me here, y’all.]

August 6

**Isaiah 12:2** (NIV) *Surely God is my salvation; I will trust and not be afraid. The LORD, the LORD himself, is my strength and my defense; he has become my salvation.*

Another, among many favorite verses, to remind me that God IS MY STRENGTH. As I put the finishing touches on this book, we are six months into the COVID-19 pandemic. No one on Earth knows what our futures will look like. I will not be afraid of tomorrow because God holds my hand. There are, no doubt, bad tomorrows ahead; but my ROCK, my ANCHOR, my STRONG TOWER, my SONG, my STRENGTH, my REFUGE, my SHELTER, my SALVATION is God Almighty. If y'all shout out "amen," it's all good!

.

August 7

**Isaiah 6:3** (NIV) *And they* [*seraphim] *were calling to one another: "Holy, holy, holy is the LORD Almighty; the whole earth is full of his glory.*

This favorite verse comes from the passage where Isaiah was commissioned by God. Isaiah had a vision and saw the Lord seated on His throne with the winged seraphim flying about Him. God is Almighty, He is Holy, and the entire earth is full of His Glory. Even though we can't see God, we can surely see the evidence of God. When I was a teenager, a Sunday School teacher explained this by saying "we can't see the wind, but we can see the evidence of the wind". If we could totally explain God, there'd be no need for faith. Faith is believing in what we cannot see, or touch – we just KNOW. And we know the Sovereign Lord. This verse not only reminds me of what God is like, it also gives me a glimpse of Heaven.

[* My interjection.]

August 8

**<u>Isaiah 41:10</u>** (NIV) *So do not fear, for I am with you; do not be dismayed, for I am your God. I will strengthen you and help you; I will uphold you with my righteous right hand.*

Another one of my favorite verses, this one says it all for me. In God we have NOTHING to fear! God is with us always, whatever may come up in our walk of life – God is there already, waiting to strengthen us, waiting to carry us, waiting to hoist us over or through whatever we face. I've known that in my head since I was a small child. But beginning in 1990, and continuing through the present day, this has finally taken up residence in my heart and has over-filled my life with peace.

August 9

**Exodus 16:14-20** (NLT) [14]*When the dew evaporated, a flaky substance as fine as frost blanketed the ground.* [15]*The Israelites were puzzled when they saw it. "What is it?" they asked each other. They had no idea what it was. And Moses told them, "It is the food the LORD has given you to eat.* [16]*These are the LORD's instructions: Each household should gather as much as it needs. Pick up two quarts for each person in your tent."* [17]*So the people of Israel did as they were told. Some gathered a lot, some only a little.* [18]*But when they measured it out, everyone had just enough. Those who gathered a lot had nothing left over, and those who gathered only a little had enough. Each family had just what it needed.* [19]*Then Moses told them, "Do not keep any of it until morning."* [20]*But some of them didn't listen and kept some of it until morning. But by then it was full of maggots and had a terrible smell. Moses was very angry with them.*

The favorite Scripture passage above speaks so clearly to the fact that God will, and does, supply our needs. We need to share with Him our requests, not because He doesn't already know, but because our sharing fosters a relationship with Him. It reminds us He is our STRENGTH and our DELIVERER. Some of the Israelites kept a portion of the bread overnight even though God had said not to do that. Basically, they didn't trust God. It's easy to judge them, but don't we do the same thing every time we worry and don't turn our problems, our whole lives, over to Him? As I write this, severe weather is forecast for our area later tonight and into the wee hours of the morning. I'm not a fan of severe weather, but I have learned to lean into God and trust Him through it. Faith over fear – always. Can I get a witness?

August 10

**<u>Jeremiah 31:3</u>** (NIV) *The LORD appeared to us in the past, saying: "I have loved you with an everlasting love; I have drawn you with unfailing kindness."*

This favorite verse reminds me of God's UNFAILING and UNCONDITIONAL love for us. No matter what, God loves us, and no matter what, He is with us. The key is recognizing His Presence and allowing Him access to our hearts. If you google "Jesus standing at the door" many images come up. Notice the door does not have a knob – the knob is on the inside. WE have to open the door to our heart, where He stands outside, knocking. He will guide us through all of our trials and tribulations. God gives us loving kindness and guidance. His Presence makes our journey bearable.

August 11

**Mark 4:39** (NIV) *He* [*Jesus] *got up, rebuked the wind and said to the waves, "Quiet! Be still!" Then the wind died down and it was completely calm.*

This favorite verse reminds me of the power God has over everything! In 2019 we visited the Sea of Galilee during our pilgrimage to Israel. Our guide explained how quickly the storms on that sea come up, giving me a much better understanding of this passage. The storms Jesus calmed in this passage, are like the storms in my life. The fear the disciples felt in that boat being rocked by the storm, are like the fears in my life. There are times when I have felt like the whole world was crashing down on me, and I'm sure there will be more times like that in my future. I get through those times by holding God's hand. God calms my soul like He calmed the sea. He guides me on this journey called life. My problems will be tolerable, and ultimately, He will guide me to Glory.

[* My interjection.]

August 12

**John 8:36** (NIV) *So if the Son sets you free, you will be free indeed.*

You might ask: set free from what? We are set free from the chains of sins through Jesus. In this favorite verse Jesus tells us that Himself. It doesn't mean we won't sin; it just means we are forgiven through Him. Remember the Garden of Eden? Adam and Eve were banished from the garden because of their sin. The whole Bible after that is God's reconciliation plan. Sin, in and of itself, separates us from God. By His GRACE and MERCY, we are restored. Shouting amen is acceptable if the Spirit so moves. Just sayin'.

August 13

**Psalm 141:8** (NIV) *But my eyes are fixed on you, Sovereign LORD; in you I take refuge—do not give me over to death.*

To me the message of this favorite verse is our focus on God, our Sovereign Lord. It's like being on a boat in the ocean and "fixing our eyes" upon a lighthouse or driving down a road and "fixing our eyes" on a landmark before us. Regardless of our lack of knowledge about that area of the ocean or city, keeping our eyes on the lighthouse or landmark ensures we get where we want/need to go. The word death at the end means evil, which equates to total and complete alienation from God.

August 14

**Psalm 102:27** (NIV) *But you remain the same, and your years will never end.*

The term "you" in this verse is referring to God, and He NEVER changes. This favorite verse reminds me that God is the One constant in my life. His promises are true, He's honest with us, He's faithful to us, He's present in our lives always. All we have to do is accept Him into our lives, and trust in His Word, reading, praying and being present with Him.

August 15

**John 17:20-23** (NIV) [20] *My prayer is not for them alone. I pray also for those who will believe in me through their message,* [21] *that all of them may be one, Father, just as you are in me and I am in you. May they also be in us so that the world may believe that you have sent me.* [22] *I have given them the glory that you gave me, that they may be one as we are one—* [23] *I in them and you in me—so that they may be brought to complete unity. Then the world will know that you sent me and have loved them even as you have loved me.*

The favorite passage above is the prayer Jesus prayed not only for the disciples that were present with Him on earth, but also to all of us that would follow Him later. This is His prayer for all of us! He prayed we'd be one, as He and God are one. Sometimes we Christians get caught up in the minutiae – immersion vs. sprinkling, confirmation vs. no confirmation, open Communion Table vs. closed Communion Table, etc. Satan loves it when that happens, because we neglect the Message LOVE ONE ANOTHER. Jesus is God's ONLY SON given for ALL OF US!

August 16

**Luke 12:25-26** (NIV) [25] *Who of you by worrying can add a single hour to your life?* [26] *Since you cannot do this very little thing, why do you worry about the rest?*

The point Jesus is making in this favorite passage is that we are incapable of adding time to our lives. Since we know we do not have that power, why worry about anything? Jesus came to shine His light on our paths and be with us always as we navigate life. In other passages He states that we will have troubles in this world, but to know that He has overcome the world! The older I get, and the more pain I see and experience, I KNOW there is NOTHING that He will not help me through. Nothing. I can't explain the peace I have from that knowledge, but I tell you this – I feel the Peace, and it makes all the difference. When the "worry bug" begins to weave its web in my life, this passage runs it off.

August 17

**<u>Proverbs 29:25</u>** (NIV) *Fear of man will prove to be a snare, but whoever trusts in the* LORD *is kept safe.*

This favorite verse points out that trusting men instead of God will get you into trouble. Fear at times makes us immobile or ineffective, because we're left waffling back and forth with ourselves as to which way to go or what to do. Trust in God eliminates the indecision from our lives as He gently leads us where He knows we are to go. My problem is that I want immediate answers. Right now. Sometimes God wants us to just sit with it a minute, perhaps to learn something we don't yet know. They (whoever "they" are), say patience is a virtue. I need to be more virtuous. Trust God and be patient. He'll lead, in HIS time.

August 18

**<u>Matthew 6:24</u>** (NIV) *No one can serve two masters. Either you will hate the one and love the other, or you will be devoted to the one and despise the other. You cannot serve both God and money.*

In this favorite verse Jesus clearly says we should focus on God. When our focus is on our relationship with God and not on ourselves or our possessions, we walk more in-tune with Him. Loving God with all our hearts means putting NOTHING before our relationship with Him. We either love God, or we don't. We either trust God, or we don't. We can't play on both sides of the fence. We must make a choice, and when we choose God, it makes all the difference in the world.

August 19

**Luke 23: 39-43** (NIV) [39] *One of the criminals who hung there hurled insults at him: "Aren't you the Messiah? Save yourself and us!"* [40] *But the other criminal rebuked him. "Don't you fear God," he said, "since you are under the same sentence?* [41] *We are punished justly, for we are getting what our deeds deserve. But this man has done nothing wrong."* [42] *Then he said, "Jesus, remember me when you come into your kingdom."* [43] *Jesus answered him, "Truly I tell you, today you will be with me in paradise."*

Many people think good deeds and work get them into Heaven. This favorite passage blows that theory out of the water. Yes, God wants us to be good people. God wants us to have good work ethics, not only in our professions but also in working to help those in need. Our relationship with God grows as we become His hands and feet on this earth. However, NOTHING we DO saves us. Only the grace and mercy of God saves us, and while deathbed conversions are not the norm, they are most certainly real.

August 20

**Genesis 50:20** (NIV) *You intended to harm me, but God intended it for good to accomplish what is now being done, the saving of many lives.*

In this favorite verse, Joseph is speaking to his brothers who many years earlier had thrown him into a pit and sold him into slavery because they were jealous of him. He was telling them how God turned that bad situation into something good. He worked his way up through the government and was now in a position to help the Israelites and his family have food during the drought. This is a lesson to us: in our darkest hours God is right there working behind the scenes to turn our tragedy into something good.

August 21

**Isaiah 41:13** (NIV) *For I am the LORD your God who takes hold of your right hand and says to you, Do not fear; I will help you.*

WOW, what a powerful verse! It's a favorite because God spoke and reminded me not to fear. He is with me. He holds my right hand, like a small child walking with a parent. Doesn't that give you peace? He is with us ALL. He will help us through ALL of our trials and tribulations. He won't leave us. With Him we have peace, we have security, we have the warmth of His love. He is our God!

August 22

**Micah 7:7** (NIV) *But as for me, I watch in hope for the* L*ORD,* *I wait for God my Savior; my God will hear me.*

As I was putting this book together from all the journals, it struck me that several of the verses were regarding God with us, God holding us, God helping us. Many of those verses were in my readings over and over again in 2012. This particular favorite verse appeared **three** times between May 9th and June 21st. God never promised us no trouble. He promised to be with us through the trouble. In retrospect, I know God was preparing me for the journey our family would take later that year in October when one of my sisters was murdered. During those dark, dark days of October 2012, we watched in hope, we waited for God our Savior, and HE HEARD US.

August 23

**2 Corinthians 1:8-9** (NIV) [8] *We do not want you to be uninformed, brothers and sisters, about the troubles we experienced in the province of Asia. We were under great pressure, far beyond our ability to endure, so that we despaired of life itself.* [9] *Indeed, we felt we had received the sentence of death. But this happened that we might not rely on ourselves but on God, who raises the dead.*

Paul reminds us in this favorite passage that it wasn't easy for them, and they suffered greatly. However, they realized even in their despair, that alone it was unbearable, but with God they could endure. This is an incredible message to all of us. GOD WILL AND DOES PROVIDE, even in our darkest hours. So many times, we allow circumstances to get in the way of our relationship and communion with God. Regardless of where we find ourselves, God is already there to be with us.

August 24

<u>**John 14:27**</u> (NIV) *Peace I leave with you; my peace I give you. I do not give to you as the world gives. Do not let your hearts be troubled and do not be afraid.*

This favorite verse initially appeared in May 2012. At the time my daughter, Jeri, and also my husband, Matthew, had medical issues that weighed heavily on my heart. This verse calmed my fears and my soul. Jesus is telling us that He's leaving us His peace. I leaned into God and trusted Him to be with me regardless of the outcomes. We will always have problems in life – no rose garden is promised for any of us. However, Christ has overcome the world, and He gives us Strength and Peace no matter what is going on around us. In seeking Him, we find Peace.

August 25

**Matthew 10:16-18** (NIV) [16] *"I am sending you out like sheep among wolves. Therefore, be as shrewd as snakes and as innocent as doves.* [17] *Be on your guard; you will be handed over to the local councils and be flogged in the synagogues.* [18] *On my account you will be brought before governors and kings as witnesses to them and to the Gentiles."*

Thankfully, in the United States, we have freedom of religion. This favorite passage reminds me of what it was like not only for the first Christians, but also the horrible conditions that still exist throughout our world in countries without freedom of worship. Jesus is being honest with His followers. Missionaries are still tortured and killed by the very people they are trying to save – the people who still don't know of God and His love. And here I sit in my warm home, in a free country, and miss so many opportunities to witness. I should be and am ashamed. We should never pass up an opportunity to share our faith. We should never take our religious freedom for granted. Never.

August 26

**1 Peter 5:6-7** (NIV) [6] *Humble yourselves, therefore, under God's mighty hand, that he may lift you up in due time.* [7] *Cast all your anxiety on him because he cares for you.*

So often life situations are thrown in our path that aren't of our making, but certainly bear down upon us and affect our lives. This favorite passage reminds me that, regardless of what life throws my way – something I've done or something someone else has done – God has my back. As I was editing this, someone let me know they were disappointed by something I did. That's like a dart straight to my heart, because I never want to disappoint anyone. What a timely passage to remind me that even in my failings, God has my back. Focusing on God and not my situations, allows me to "cast my cares (anxiety) on Him" and rest in His love and peace no matter what. Amen.

August 27

**<u>Luke 1:37</u>** (CSB) *"For nothing will be impossible with God."*

This favorite verse spells it out plainly that nothing is impossible with God. Luke is speaking specifically about the virgin birth, but, come on – virgin birth, parting of the Red Sea, raising Lazarus and Christ from the dead, just to name three miracles; you really think there is anything God can't do? Now you may argue, well then why is there pain in the world? Why sickness? Why hatefulness, bullying, war, etc? That's on us! Mankind didn't stick to God's plan. The Garden of Eden would still be going strong had Adam and Eve just stuck to the Plan. God did not create puppets, God created people, and the people chose to turn their backs on Him. Even in our darkest hours when God doesn't heal our loved ones on this earth, or when someone we love is murdered, or when evil people shoot up schools and other places, or when war breaks out due to evil people – EVEN THEN, God who allows us to be free to choose, is working in the background to bring good out of the bad, to bring comfort to those affected, and to bring love to this loveless world.

August 28

**Revelation 12:10** (NIV) *Then I heard a loud voice in heaven say: "Now have come the salvation and the power and the kingdom of our God, and the authority of his Messiah. For the accuser of our brothers and sisters, who accuses them before our God day and night, has been hurled down."*

This favorite verse is speaking of God's ultimate and final victory over Satan. I really like the term "hurled down". Can I get an amen? We can win battles with Satan in our daily journeys with God, but we must be diligent to keep our focus ON God! As we lean on God and allow Him to guide our steps, we are able to resist Satan. We, like Jesus, can utter the words "get thee behind me, Satan". (Memorized that one from the KJV, but you get the drift.) It is very hard for Satan to get into our lives when we are walking faithfully with God, our Shield and Strength against the evil one.

August 29

**<u>Luke 1:76-79</u>** (NIV) [76] *"And you, my child, will be called a prophet of the Most High; for you will go before the Lord to prepare the way for him,* [77] *to give his people the knowledge of salvation through the forgiveness of their sin,* [78] *because of the tender mercy of our God, by which the rising sun will come to us from heaven* [79] *to shine on those living in darkness and in the shadow of death, to guide our feet into the path of peace."*

This favorite passage is a part of Zechariah's song regarding his and Elizabeth's son, John the Baptist. It's as applicable to us as it was when it was first sung. God shines His Light on us to show us the way. If we trust Him, and stay tuned into Him, our paths will be clear, and He will walk with us every step of the way. It's as easy as turning on your flashlight in the dark of night to find your way. Take advantage of this Resource our God provides.

August 30

**<u>Isaiah 55:8-9</u>** (NIV) [8] *"For my thoughts are not your thoughts, neither are your ways my ways," declares the* L*ORD.* [9] *"As the heavens are higher than the earth, so are my ways higher than your ways and my thoughts than your thoughts."*

I love this favorite passage because simply put, it points out that God is God, and we are not. His ways and thoughts are higher than ours. The only way to connect with Him is through a RELATIONSHIP with Him. We call or text our friends and family 50 times a day. God is our Father. He'd like to hear from us. Prayer is communicating with God. A dear friend once said, "Prayer doesn't change things, prayer changes people." That is SO true. Our prayer life deepens our relationship with God as we share everything – including the times we're angry with Him. Yes, God has heard and listened to many a hissy-fit (I'm Southern, deal with it.) from me. Guess what? He loves me anyway. Time in prayer, time in Scripture study, and time being still/quiet and listening for the "still small Voice" all bring us closer to the Living God.

August 31

**John 14:5-6** (NIV) [5] *Thomas said to him, "Lord, we don't know where you are going, so how can we know the way?"* [6] *Jesus answered, "I am the way and the truth and the life. No one comes to the Father except through me."*

Jesus had been talking with the disciples about preparing a place [Heaven] for them, and that they'd know the way. Thomas (pretty sure he and I are kindred spirits) pipes up and asks, "how do we know that?" Jesus basically said, "You know Me, you know The Way." Well, duh. How easy is that? This passage is a favorite because Jesus spells out for people like Thomas (and me) that He is the Way! As Paul Davis once said, "When we fly on an airplane, we trust that the pilot knows the way!" Jesus is out Pilot through life. When we have a relationship with God/Jesus – One in the same – we know the Way. And when we know the Way, God is our core, the center of our lives, and no matter what is swirling on around us, we have Peace.

September 1

**<u>Colossians 2:2-3</u>** (NIV) [2] *My goal is that they may be encouraged in heart and united in love, so that they may have the full riches of complete understanding, in order that they may know the mystery of God, namely, Christ,* [3] *in whom are hidden all the treasures of wisdom and knowledge.*

Paul's purpose in this favorite passage was to encourage and unite the church, so that in unity the people could seek and find the full and complete gifts of Christ. Christ is the sure foundation for our lives, a rich store of salvation, wisdom, and knowledge. We, as the church, should BE THE CHURCH. We should do all we can to show the world by our lives who Christ is. Sadly, many churches are getting so caught up in their differences of opinion, that they are losing sight of WHY we are the church. We are here to spread the Gospel – the Good News of Jesus Christ! Let's get busy. Can I get a witness?

September 2

**Zephaniah 3:17** (NLT) *For the LORD your God is living among you. He is a mighty savior. He will take delight in you with gladness. With his love, he will calm all your fears. He will rejoice over you with joyful songs.*

This favorite verse reiterates God's Presence in our lives. NO MATTER WHAT, God is with us. Even in our screw-ups, His love is like no other and He reaches out to us. It is my comfort and Strength that God is with me always. My prayer is that if you haven't already done so, you will accept His Gift of Salvation. If you have already done so, my prayer is that you will allow the peace and love of God to calm you. Share that Peace and Love with others every day of your life.

September 3

**Romans 13:11-14** (MSG) [11-14] *But make sure that you don't get so absorbed and exhausted in taking care of all your day-by-day obligations that you lose track of the time and doze off, oblivious to God. The night is about over, dawn is about to break. Be up and awake to what God is doing! God is putting the finishing touches on the salvation work he began when we first believed. We can't afford to waste a minute, must not squander these precious daylight hours in frivolity and indulgence, in sleeping around and dissipation, in bickering and grabbing everything in sight. Get out of bed and get dressed! Don't loiter and linger, waiting until the very last minute. Dress yourselves in Christ, and be up and about!*

In this favorite passage, Paul is telling the church to stay focused on God even in their busy schedule. He's reminding us to put God first in our lives, and not to get so caught up in doing things, even good things, that we lose sight of Him. This is why the Bible is still relevant today, to us. These words written in the first century are just as spot-on today as they were the day they were penned! God wants us up and about dressed for life, not wallowing in self-pity, or so busy we forget Whose we are. We are His children. Let us all live out our faith.

September 4

**Acts 17:28** (NIV) *"For in him we live and move and have our being. As some of your own poets have said, 'We are his offspring."*

This favorite verse reminds me that in God I live and move. In Him I become who I was created to be. I'm His daughter. In our weaknesses and shortcomings God works and gives us His Strength. Everything we do is related to how we live and move within Him. We are to root ourselves in Him in order to grow into who He created us to be. We are in Him, He is in us. Can I get an amen?

September 5

**Luke 23:32-38** (NLT) *[32]Two others, both criminals, were led out to be executed with him. [33]When they came to a place called The Skull, they nailed him to the cross. And the criminals were also crucified—one on his right and one on his left. [34]Jesus said, "Father, forgive them, for they don't know what they are doing." And the soldiers gambled for his clothes by throwing dice. [35]The crowd watched and the leaders scoffed. "He saved others," they said, "let him save himself if he is really God's Messiah, the Chosen One." [36]The soldiers mocked him, too, by offering him a drink of sour wine. [37]They called out to him, "If you are the King of the Jews, save yourself!" [38]A sign was fastened above him with these words: "This is the King of the Jews."*

So many times in our lives people hurt us and make us angry, and we build up animosity toward them. We hold grudges. This favorite passage clearly describes Jesus' reaction to being wronged: "Father, forgive them". Jesus followed through with God's Plan of the crucifixion in spite of the physical and emotional torture, to redeem us – who did NOTHING to deserve redemption. And, He forgave, not only them, but also us. And the two thieves? One of them (see verses 41-43) realized Jesus was Who He said He was, and received the blessing of eternal life. Notice his forgiveness did not erase the consequences of his actions. Just because we forgive someone, or they forgive us, it doesn't erase the consequences. If it's a friend or family member, it doesn't necessarily mean our relationship will be restored. It just means our hearts are not dark with unforgiveness. We forgive because God has forgiven us, and in doing so gives us the ability to forgive others. How dare we hold grudges and not forgive.

September 6

**<u>Hebrews 13:15</u>** (NIV) *Through Jesus, therefore, let us continually offer to God a sacrifice of praise—the fruit of lips that openly profess his name.*

As we go through our daily walk, we are to always openly profess our faith in Christ. If we're invested in God and His Word, then our lives should be a living testament of that. By living our faith, we reach everyone who crosses our paths. I remember as a teenager in the youth area of our church, a sign that read something like: "I can't hear what you're saying, because your actions are screaming something different." Our lips, and our lives should always reflect Whose we are. This favorite verse clearly reminds us of that.

September 7

**Exodus 20:3** (NIV) *You shall have no other gods before me.*

We are to worship God, and Him alone. You may say, “well, duh, Debi, I believe in God not some idol,” and you’d be correct. When this commandment was given to Moses, I’m sure it was meant for the Israelites not to worship the pagan gods in that area. However, I’m also sure this favorite verse speaks to us today about NOT making things in our lives more important than God. We may not purposely put something else ahead of God, but Satan has a sneaky way of tricking us into doing just that. Things we own, things we enjoy doing – all of these can, and sometimes do, become “idols” of sorts because they prevent us from putting God first. The best way to ensure this doesn’t happen is to cultivate and maintain a strong relationship with God.

September 8

**Isaiah 60:2** (NIV) *See, darkness covers the earth and thick darkness is over the peoples, but the LORD rises upon you and his glory appears over you.*

This favorite verse is a reminder to us that God's creation is full of Light, because God rises upon us! Isn't that the most wonderful analogy? Even in our darkest moments, God rises above our situation and covers us in His light and love. He will bring us out of our darkness. Sometimes the way out, is ***through***. He walks with us and even carries us **through** our darkness. God calls us to action in the Light to help others along the way as well. We never know when our story might be exactly what someone struggling needs to hear. Let's share our journey, y'all.

September 9

**<u>Matthew 28:18</u>** (NIV) *Then Jesus came to them and said, "All authority in heaven and on earth has been given to me."*

Jesus is God; therefore, all God is, He is – having the authority in heaven and in earth. Jesus speaks clearly in this favorite verse. We are to enter into a relationship with Him, praising Him for Who He is, and for what He has done and will do. In doing so, we come to understand His will for our lives, as we walk with Him daily. We become better people. We become who we were created to be.

September 10

**<u>Revelation 2:4</u>** (NIV) *Yet I hold this against you: You have forsaken the love you had at first.*

This favorite verse is God speaking to the church of Ephesus. In verses 1-3, the church is praised for the good works that they have done; however, in all their efforts, the key to God is missing: LOVE. They have somehow bogged themselves down doing this and that and have forgotten WHO they are serving. God is love, and all we do for Him should be based upon our love for Him and our love for others. Doing otherwise is futile. We must remember tolove as we travel our life’s road.

September 11

**<u>Romans 8:6</u>** (NIV) *The mind governed by the flesh is death, but the mind governed by the Spirit is life and peace.*

This favorite verse reminds me to be governed by the Spirit Who dwells in me. As long as I focus on God, I have peace in my life, even though the turmoil of daily life surrounds me. God guards and guides my steps always. I'm never alone. No one living in America in 2001, can see the date "September 11", and not remember the horror of that day. Some people dared to ask where God was that day. I cringed when I heard that question, because I knew God was where God always is – with us. Every. Step. Of. The. Way. Pure evil was at work that day. Evil that is incomprehensible to most of us. I felt great sorrow for our country during that time, and I felt great sorrow for those asking where God was. Peace and true happiness come from God – there is no other Source. My life has proven this over and over again, and because I know this, I share my journey. I'm not even close to being perfect or having all the answers. Sometimes I don't even know the questions! Regardless of this, my life is filled with peace from the Spirit of God. Amen.

September 12

**Galatians 5:22-23** (NLT) [22] *But the Holy Spirit produces this kind of fruit in our lives: love, joy, peace, patience, kindness, goodness, faithfulness,* [23] *gentleness and self-control. There is no law against these things!*

Oh, to be the person who lives out the "fruit of the Spirit" daily, as listed in this favorite passage. I'm definitely not there!! But the goal is there for me to achieve. I just have to rest in Christ and become more like Him – every second, every minute, every hour, every day. MORE LIKE HIM. Diving into His Word daily. Spending time in prayer with Him daily. Focusing on Whose I am daily. Y'all with me?

September 13

**1 Peter 2:9** (NIV) *But you are a chosen people, a royal priesthood, a holy nation, God's special possession, that you may declare the praises of him who called you out of darkness into his wonderful light.*

This favorite verse reminds us we are CHOSEN. Royal Priesthood. Holy Nation. God's special possession. Doesn't that give you chills?! God loves us unconditionally, and I am so grateful for that as I fall short of who He created me to be. This verse reminds me, He chose me anyway! He has brought me out of darkness and into His light. It is an honor to be His child, and with His guidance and love we can be a beacon to others to know Him. Who's with me?

September 14

**<u>Psalm 130:5</u>** (NIV) *I wait for the LORD, my whole being waits, and in his word I put my hope.*

WOW! This favorite verse touches my soul so fiercely. "My whole being waits…in His Word I put my hope." The magnitude of the verse shakes me to my core. God is unseen. Faith is the key to knowing God. Looking around us we find God's work everywhere. Miracles abound. His majestic beauty paints our countrysides. Stars paint our skies. I will wait on the Lord, and in Him I will put my trust – always. Can I get an amen?

.

September 15

**<u>Proverbs 31:25</u>** (NIV) *She is clothed with strength and dignity; she can laugh at the days to come.*

This favorite verse comes from the passage that describes a virtuous woman. As I've said before, it behooves us to read the whole passage to completely understand a single verse, so I encourage you to do so. Verse 25 is the epitome of a successful, happy woman. I'm not talking monetarysuccess; I'm talking about being content with who and where she is in life. With God's help, strength and dignity will work together in our personalities to give us love, laughter, and a life well-lived. A virtuous woman is a Godly woman. And it's not just about women. A virtuous person is a Godly person. Can I get a witness?

September 16

**Proverbs 16:9** (NIV) *In their hearts, humans plan their course, but the LORD establishes their steps.*

This favorite verse reminds me that our plans are governed by God, as we walk the path He has led us to. When God is in the equation of our daily lives, His will is part of what we choose to do through communion with Him. We make our plans based upon our heart's desires, and upon the prayerful contemplation of the options before us. As we walk toward our goals, the Lord plans out our steps and guides us onward. That sure works for me. How 'bout y'all?

September 17

**Jude 24-25** (NIV) [24] *To him who is able to keep you from stumbling and to present you before his glorious presence without fault and with great joy— [25] to the only God our Savior be glory, majesty, power and authority, through Jesus Christ our Lord, before all ages, now and forevermore! Amen.*

Many pastors use these favorite verses as a benediction at the end of their services. They remind us that we are to give Jesus the glory, always. He directs our paths. He keeps us from stumbling when we allow Him to be with us. And when we push on without Him, He catches us when we fall. Through Him we are able to stand before God without blemish, because Jesus has paid the price. Amen.

September 18

**<u>Psalm 8:1-4</u>** (NLT) *[1]O LORD, our Lord, your majestic name fills the earth! Your glory is higher than the heavens. [2]You have taught children and infants to tell of your strength, silencing your enemies and all who oppose you. [3]When I look at the night sky and see the work of your fingers—the moon and the stars you set in place—[4]what are mere mortals that you should think about them, human beings that you should care for them?*

These favorite verses remind me of God's creation shouting His glory always. Infants gurgling and toddlers singing praise songs drown out the hate in the world. The laughter of children playing, the joy of teens and adults joking around with each other are all reminders of the good in this world. God's glory is everywhere, and even in the midst of pain, suffering and struggling, we find Him. The writer of the Psalm describes all the majesty and glory and is in awe that God is the Master of the Universe, and still cares for us. Oh yes, He does – amen and amen.

September 19

**Matthew 10:24-25** (NIV) [24] *"The student is not above the teacher, nor a servant above his master.* [25] *It is enough for students to be like their teachers, and servants like their masters. If the head of the house has been called Beelzebub, how much more the members of his household!"*

At first glance you may wonder what in the world Jesus is saying in this favorite passage. Basically, He's reminding us how He was treated on this earth by not only the Government officials of the day, but also the religious leaders of the day. So, when we're made fun of or mocked, remember these verses, and know that Jesus is with us always. Even Jesus was mocked and made fun of. We are to persevere through it all, and rest in the assurance that Jesus knows how we feel, and He will get us through. We're not promised a rose garden. We ARE promised a God Who is with us and understands the pain among our thorns.

September 20

**Deuteronomy 31:6** (NIV) [6] *"Be strong and courageous. Do not be afraid or terrified because of them, for the LORD your God goes with you; he will never leave you nor forsake you."*

This favorite verse says we are to be courageous, knowing God will never leave us. When we don't trust Him it breaks His heart, much the same way children in our lives break our hearts when they choose a path other than God's path. Another example is when we're teaching a child in our lives to ride a bike, we stay with them running down the road beside them lest they fall. That's how God is with us – running right along beside us. That image of God makes me smile. He won't leave us. Ever.

September 21

**John 8:31-32** (NIV) [31] *To the Jews who had believed him, Jesus said, "If you hold to my teaching, you are really my disciples.* [32] *Then you will know the truth, and the truth will set you free."*

This favorite passage explains who Jesus' disciples are. To be a true disciple of Jesus, we must hold true to His teachings and to His Word. Studying Scripture and making notes as to what it says to us, reading other materials, and attending Bible studies, help us discern the message God is speaking to us. Living in the message we have received, sets us free from a life without God.

September 22

**<u>Deuteronomy 33:*12*</u>** (NIV) *"About Benjamin he said: Let the beloved of the LORD rest secure in him, for he shields him all day long, and the one the LORD loves rests between his shoulders."*

Many times in my life I have imagined myself climbing up into God's lap and just being held by Him. The security and peace I felt in those moments is the most cherished feeling there is. And just like Benjamin, we can rest between the shoulders of God! This favorite verse reminds me of a daddy carrying his child through a crowd. Did your daddy ever do that? Mine did. Every parade, every fairground, every large crowd. I was always on his back. God is our Heavenly Daddy, and we are welcomed to ride on His back. Can I get an amen?

September 23

**<u>Titus 3:5</u>** (NIV) *he saved us, not because of righteous things we had done, but because of his mercy. He saved us through the washing of rebirth and renewal by the Holy Spirit,*

It saddens me that so many people fail to embrace this favorite verse. Our salvation is a TOTAL AND COMPLETE GIFT FROM GOD. It has nothing to do with anything we have done, or how good we are. It's only and solely because of God's mercy and grace. He sent His only Son, Jesus, to take on the sins of the world. I heard a song with words something like: "not because of who I am, but because of what He's done; not because of what I've done, but because of Who He is". That's it y'all. It's God, not us. All we have to do is accept His Gift. Amen and amen.

September 24

**John 4:23-24** (NIV) [23] *"Yet a time is coming and has now come when the true worshipers will worship the Father in the Spirit and in truth, for they are the kind of worshipers the Father seeks.* [24] *God is spirit, and his worshipers must worship in the Spirit and in truth."*

In this favorite passage Jesus speaks of how we are to worship God. God is Spirit, and as such we worship Him in Spirit and in truth. We give ourselves totally to Him and He accepts us as we are. He refines us as the jeweler refines the jewel. Everything we accomplish is of and from God – we are nothing without Him. God as the Holy Spirit lives in our souls. Remember to be a good host. Just sayin'.

September 25

**John 4:16-18** (NIV) [16] *He told her, "Go, call your husband and come back."* [17] *"I have no husband," she replied. Jesus said to her, "You are right when you say you have no husband.* [18] *The fact is, you have had five husbands, and the man you now have is not your husband. What you have just said is quite true."*

It is a comfort and at the same time an unsettling thing when we realize God knows our every thought, action, and motive. He KNOWS our true selves – no hiding from His Truth. It's a comfort because our loving Father knows us. It's unsettling because our loving Father knows we are not always loving. For instance: getting cut off in traffic, at the height of a competition, war, petty disagreements – the list is endless. In this favorite passage, Jesus KNEW the woman at the well, just as He knows us. The Psalmist prayed "search my heart, O God." God does search our hearts, and since He does, let's make an effort to keep our hearts pure. As a result, our actions will also be pure because they are a reflection of our hearts. We typically clean house when we're expecting guests. God lives within us. Let's keep the house of our soul clean for our Lord.

September 26

**John 15:9-12** (NLT) [9] *"I have loved you even as the Father has loved me. Remain in my love. [10] When you obey my commandments, you remain in my love, just as I obey my Father's commandments and remain in his love. [11] I have told you these things so that you will be filled with my joy. Yes, your joy will overflow! [12] This is my commandment: Love each other in the same way I have loved you."*

In this favorite passage, Jesus is explaining to us that true love, true peace, true joy is completed and perfected in the love of the Father. Jesus loves us like God loves Him. He commands us to love each other like He loves us. It's very simple, and straightforward. And yet, we – yes, I said we – want to add addendums to it because some of us only want to love those just like us. There are NO addendums, y'all.

September 27

**Deuteronomy 30:19b-20** (NIV) *choose life, so that you and your children may live* [20] *and that you may love the LORD your God, listen to his voice, and hold fast to him. For the LORD is your life, and he will give you many years in the land he swore to give to your fathers, Abraham, Isaac and Jacob.*

These favorite verses are clear, that by choosing God we choose life. Without God there is no life. I can't even imagine my life without His presence. We are created in His image and are only complete in Him. We are created with souls to commune with God. When we renew our minds in Him, and hold fast to His teachings, we either see clearly what He would have us do, or we are content in His Presence until the path is revealed. I know I may sound like a broken record, but for me it's God, and God alone.

September 28

**Exodus 20:4-5** (NIV) [4] *"You shall not make for yourself an image in the form of anything in heaven above or on the earth beneath or in the waters below.* [5] *You shall not bow down to them or worship them; for I, the LORD your God, am a jealous God, punishing the children for the sin of the parents to the third and fourth generation of those who hate me."*

These favorite verses remind us that we are not to make idols of any kind, and we are only to worship God. Most of us haven't made graven images or idols, and most of us worship God – or do we? I once heard you can read your checkbook register (yes, I still keep one) and that shows who/what you love and worship – because obviously, that's what you spend your money on. Whatever is first in our lives is what/who we worship. Cars, video games, any entertainment that we put above God, knocks Him out of first place in our lives. Be careful, be mindful, and always have God first and all the other people/things in life with fall into place.

September 29

<u>**Ephesians 2:6-8**</u> (NIV) [6] *And God raised us up with Christ and seated us with him in the heavenly realms in Christ Jesus,* [7] *in order that in the coming ages he might show the incomparable riches of his grace, expressed in his kindness to us in Christ Jesus.* [8] *For it is by grace you have been saved, through faith—and this is not from yourselves, it is the gift of God—*

This favorite passage says as a result of our salvation, we have been raised up in Christ and seated with Him in the heavenly realms **in order that** we may experience the incomparable riches of God's grace. Keeping our eyes, thoughts, and our whole being fixed on Him ensures our love and peace. And yes, we experience much of this right here on earth because Christ dwells in us and us in Him. His grace, His gifts are here and now. Grab on. Hold on. The ride ***with*** God is amazing!

September 30

**Psalm 40:1-3** (NIV) [1]*I waited patiently for the* L*ORD; he turned to me and heard my cry.* [2] *He lifted me out of the slimy pit, out of the mud and mire; he set my feet on a rock and gave me a firm place to stand.* [3] *He put a new song in my mouth, a hymn of praise to our God. Many will see and fear the* LORD *and put their trust in him.*

The Psalms have always soothed my soul. This beautiful favorite passage tells of how God turns to us and helps us out of our despair. How He lifts us out of the slimy pit – the mud and the mire. Have y'all ever experienced this? I have. The word "fear" in the next to the last sentence means to revere or show reverence to, instead of being fearful of. I thank God and bless His name that He walks with me every step of the way, and carries me in many, many cases. Praise be to God.

October 1

**<u>Ephesians 6:14-16</u>** (NIV) [14] *Stand firm then, with the belt of truth buckled around your waist, with the breastplate of righteousness in place,* [15] *and with your feet fitted with the readiness that comes from the gospel of peace.* [16] *In addition to all this, take up the shield of faith, with which you can extinguish all the flaming arrows of the evil one.*

As we travel this life, we encounter many bad things. Not only temptations, but also just pure evil as Satan prevails in the lives of many and they rain terror on the rest of us. This favorite passage speaks to my heart about the strength we find in God. Faith in Christ squashes* any uprising Satan may hurl our way. The very mention of God's name sends Satan packing. So, as we encounter attacks, stand firm, dressing ourselves in the whole armor of God as described above. I'm telling y'all, God has your back!

**[or squushes, if you prefer, but that spelling looks funny to me. Let the record show my spell-check's head just exploded.]*

October 2

**Exodus 3:14** (NIV) *God said to Moses, "I AM WHO I AM. This is what you are to say to the Israelites: 'I AM has sent me to you.'"*

God is the Great **I AM** Who needs no other introduction. The Israelites were enslaved in Egypt when God chose Moses to lead them to the land He had promised Abraham. Even though they had embraced some of the Egyptian culture, they all knew in their hearts Who **I AM** is. I believe that's true today, and if we who profess to know would not only speak of Him, but also live like we knew Him, then we could change the world! As this favorite verse says, the Great I AM has sent us; let us go forth and reflect His love. Dr. David Campbell, pastor at Due West UMC at this writing, did an entire series entitled "Be the Church". I say, "let the being begin". Can I get an amen?

October 3

**John 8:12** (NIV) [12] *When Jesus spoke again to the people, he said, "I am the light of the world. Whoever follows me will never walk in darkness, but will have the light of life."*

This favorite verse contains one of the I AM phrases of Jesus. I AM is a reference to Exodus 3:14 from yesterday. Jesus says that He is the Light of the world. As His followers we are to be like Him and live in His Light and shine His Light on others. Christian means "Christlike" – pretty self-explanatory. There are many Christians who act anything but Christlike. That to me is incomprehensible. How can we who KNOW, live as if we don't? We who follow Christ must immerse ourselves into His Word. We must reflect His Light and His Love to all who come in contact with us. In Matthew 5:14 (NIV), Jesus says "You are the light of the world, a city on a hill cannot be hidden." Do you remember the Flintstones' cartoons and how the city lit up at night? Well, that's us, y'all. We need to step up, light up, and lead people to Christ with our actions. Living out the life He has prepared for us. Be the Light of Christ!

October 4

**<u>Romans 12:12</u>** (NIV) *Be joyful in hope, patient in affliction, faithful in prayer.*

Well, there you go, this favorite verse is short, sweet, and to the point. Praise God, He cares for us and loves us. When we face situations that break our hearts, or that anger us – HE IS THERE! He has overcome the evil of this world. He will help us through. Take hold of the hope that He offers. Learn His patience and feel His presence. Study His Word, and prayerfully seek His will in your life. Anchor yourself to God. I anchored myself to God on October 4, 1959, when, at the age of six, I walked the aisle of Log Cabin Baptist Church in Macon, GA, and made my public profession of faith in Jesus Christ. That one act, the faith of a six-year-old child, has made all the difference in my life. Amen and amen.

October 5

**Psalm 46:10** (NIV) *He says, "Be still, and know that I am God; I will be exalted among the nations, I will be exalted in the earth."*

**Numbers 6:24-26** (NIV) [24] *'"The LORD bless you and keep you;* [25] *the LORD make his face shine on you and be gracious to you;* [26] *the LORD turn his face toward you and give you peace."'*

The above Psalm was written by the Sons of Korah, and the passage from Numbers, is God speaking to Moses about what Moses is to tell Aaron and his sons regarding how to bless the Israelites. Both were written decades before Christ was born, which means both were written well over 1,953 years before I was born. Yet both are favorite verses of mine. Both are as relevant today as the day they were first penned. Both of these passages appeared in my daily devotion eight days after we found out that my sister, Gail, had been murdered. Eight. Days. I wrote that day: ***The verses above are such a comfort and a reminder of God's love always; and in these difficult days how He is carrying us and loving us.*** The same God Who spoke through the Sons of Korah and through Moses, spoke to me in October 2012. The same God Who speaks to all of us today. Amen and amen.

October 6

**<u>1 John 2:28</u>** (NIV) *And now, dear children, continue in him, so that when he appears we may be confident and unashamed before him at his coming.*

Growing up in the Southern Baptist Church, we were reminded to live our lives as if Christ's return was this very day. As I write this, I'm in my late sixties and that one statement has stuck with me all these years. I must admit I don't always live like that (I'm pretty much a teenager in God years). However, I always know I should, and that knowledge brings me around to remorse and repentance. This favorite verse reminds me to live like I'm dying, because we all are. Christ is our Anchor. If we tether ourselves to Him, even though we may begin to drift in choppy waters of life, we can pull ourselves back to Him by focusing on what we know to be the Truth.

.

October 7

**John 13:34-35** (NIV)[34] *"A new command I give you: Love one another. As I have loved you, so you must love one another. [35] By this everyone will know that you are my disciples, if you love one another."*

In this favorite passage Jesus is giving us a command to love one another. It isn't a suggestion; it is a command. This command is just as relevant to the church today, as it was when Jesus said it. There are many difficult issues facing the Church today. The term "church" refers to the body of Christ – all Christians, regardless of denomination. Many Christians are at odds with one another over various social issues, and the harsh arguments are hurting the Kingdom, not uniting the Kingdom. Both sides bear the responsibility to do ALL THEY DO IN LOVE, and sadly, both sides are missing the mark in many cases. My heart breaks, my heart hurts. As I began to write today, I stumbled upon a quote by John Wesley: "Though we cannot think alike, may we not love alike? May we not be of one heart, though we are not of one opinion? Without all doubt, we may. Herein all the children of God may unite, notwithstanding these smaller differences." Can I get an amen?

October 8

**Matthew 28:20b** (NIV) *"And surely I am with you always, to the very end of the age."*

Jesus is speaking to His disciples in this favorite verse, but this is a message intended for all who follow Him. He is a part of who we are by the power of the Holy Spirit in us. His peace and love fill our very being. We are never alone or forsaken by God. Regardless of our situation, regardless of what we're doing or where we are, God is with us ALWAYS! Doesn't that just give y'all peace? As I get older, fewer things scare me; well, let me rephrase that: Fewer things in real life scare me. (I still do not watch scary movies, or read scary books, because neither is done easily with one's eyes closed.) Seriously, though, the bad/scary things life throws our way are nothing compared to God's love. Really. No. Contest. Praise God.

October 9

**<u>John 7:38</u>** (NIV) *"Whoever believes in me, as Scripture has said, rivers of living water will flow from within them."*

When we accept Christ as our Lord and Savior, the streams of living water do flow within us. Jesus tells us Himself in this favorite verse. As He explained to the woman at the well*, the waters He gives aren't just to quench our thirst at the moment, but to forever quench our thirst for God. I have felt these living waters many times as I have walked the valleys of this life. The living waters of Christ lead to eternal life. I don't know how people navigate life without God, and the living water. In science we learn that water flowing over rocks molds the rocks into what they become over the years. God's living water molds us in the same way. Amen.

**[see John 4:1-13]*

October 10

**Proverbs 12:18** (NIV) *The words of the reckless pierce like swords, but the tongue of the wise brings healing.*

When I was younger, it was so easy for me just to spout off at someone rather than listen to what they were saying. When our words are reckless, we can cut someone to the core. God gave us two ears and one mouth for a reason. We must listen carefully to what someone is saying, and hear their heart, not just their words. Slow to speak – listen and pray first; then what comes from our mouths will be wholesome. Not only will this be a blessing to whomever we're interacting with, but it will also teach those watching us a better way to respond rather than just reacting. This one fact has come home to me since becoming a grandmother. Setting good examples for the younger generation is critical. Our Holy Father is saying "watch your mouth." Our response is, "Okay, Daddy."

October 11

**John 14:1** (NIV) *"Do not let your hearts be troubled. You believe in God; believe also in me."*

In this favorite verse Jesus tells us not to let our hearts be troubled. This verse was my devotion on July 28, 2015. July 28th is significant because it's my sister Gail's birthday. She had been gone almost three years on the day God gave me this verse. God knew how sad I am every year because she's no longer on earth for me to celebrate with her. He knew the hole I have in my heart every July 28$^{th}$. He gave me this scripture that day as a reminder that He is always with me. I pray as you walk the path of your life and as you encounter the pains and injustices of this life, you always remember God is with you and you need not be troubled.

October 12

**<u>Psalm 37:7</u>** (NIV) *Be still before the* LORD *and wait patiently for him; do not fret when people succeed in their ways, when they carry out their wicked schemes.*

This amazing favorite verse, written over 500 years BEFORE Jesus was born - so well over 2500 years ago - is just as appropriate today as when it was written. Our country went through the longest shutdown of the Federal Government in its history just a few years ago. I was so angry that our elected officials would hold innocent civilians hostage just to get their way! Many years ago, as a single mom, I was directly affected by another needless federal government shutdown. And only through my faith did I weather that storm. It was a trying time for me. And without my faith, I have no idea how I would have handled it. Only through faith will any of us weather the ridiculous and meaningless things that occasionally happen in life. Be still before the Lord. He's got our backs.

October 13

**<u>Job 13:15</u>** (NIV) *Though he slay me, yet will I hope in him; I will surely defend my ways to his face.*

The words in this favorite verse seem to indicate that Job thought his problems came from God, but even so he still had hope in the Lord. He still had such a relationship with God that he felt comfortable defending himself to God. I make huge mistakes and have done so for 68+ years as I write this. God loves me anyway. The troubles I've experienced in life did not, in my opinion, come from God, but I know He used them as teaching moments for me. I'm a slow learner, but God is patient with me. And, like Job, I talk honestly with God. I've been known to defend myself to Him. I'm not bold, I'm just a child of God loved by God. I'm comfortable enough in that love to have an honest conversation with Him.

October 14

**Matthew 7:24-25** (NIV) [24] *"Therefore everyone who hears these words of mine and puts them into practice is like a wise man who built his house on the rock.* [25] *The rain came down, the streams rose, and the winds blew and beat against that house; yet it did not fall, because it had its foundation on the rock.*

When I was a child, we used to sing a little song in Sunday School about this parable. Some of the words were: "The rains came down, but the house stood firm." As I've mentioned before, any time Jesus said "therefore" it means as a result of what I've said earlier, you do this. When I read this favorite passage, I think of a boat anchored in place, so that it doesn't drift and get beaten up during a storm. As we tether ourselves to God, like a boat anchored properly for a storm, the storms of life will be much easier to bear. Jesus is the Rock of Ages, and He has assured us that He's with us through all the storms of life.

.

October 15

**2 Corinthians 5:21** (NIV) *God made him who had no sin to be sin for us, so that in him we might become the righteousness of God.*

He became sin for us. Five words that pack a powerful punch in this favorite verse! Do you see what that means?! God, the very Creator of this world became HUMAN so we would have an example ***like us*** to follow in order to become more like God. He neutralizes the sin brought on by Adam and Eve, and makes us able to have a relationship with God that they robbed us of because of their actions in the Garden. To complete that process, the one and only perfect human, Jesus Christ, took on every sin imaginable as He hung on that cross. He was fully God (perfect) and fully man so that He could carry every sin committed on this planet and thereby make us white as snow.

October 16

**Ephesians 5:15-16** (NIV) *Be very careful, then, how you live—not as unwise but as wise, [16] making the most of every opportunity, because the days are evil.*

We are to walk this journey of life using the wisdom the good Lord has given us. He lights our path with His Word. He gives us strength when we are weak. He guides us with urgings from the Holy Spirit. We just need to be focused and stay focused on Him as this favorite passage says. When we stray it's so easy to fall prey to the evil of the world. Being a person with ADHD, I can use humor and say sometimes God must look down at His creation and all we little ADHD people running all around must remind Him of trying to herd cats. However, it's not just we ADHD people straying, it's the whole world. Be mindful of your choices and stay focused on God. He is our Shepherd, and He calls us by name. Listen to Him. Follow Him.

October 17

**Isaiah 42:3** (NIV) *A bruised reed he will not break, and a smoldering wick he will not snuff out. In faithfulness he will bring forth justice.*

It seems to me that in this favorite verse, Isaiah is saying God won't break us when we're down, but will bring us into Truth. The reason I believe that, is the many times in my life that things have been so bleak I felt I'd break, and yet the Light (God) in my life would not allow the breaking to happen. Out of the chaos, I always learned something about myself and something about God that made the trying times worth the journey.

October 18

**<u>Psalm 32:7</u>** (NIV) You are my hiding place; you will protect me from trouble and surround me with songs of deliverance.

**<u>Psalm 55:17</u>** (NIV) *Evening, morning and noon I cry out in distress, and he hears my voice.*

**<u>Psalm 62:8</u>** (NIV) *Trust in him at all times, you people; pour out your hearts to him, for God is our refuge.*

I realize I don't usually list several verses from different chapters, but all of them are favorites, and speak to my soul so deeply that I had to share them. They remind me of God's closeness and complete involvement in my life. All hours of the day. Trusting Him. Praying to Him. Following Him. Resting in Him. HE is Who propels me through life and carries me through the muddle when I can't put one foot in front of the other.

October 19

**2 Samuel 12:1-10** (NLT) [1]*So the LORD sent Nathan the prophet to tell David this story: "There were two men in a certain town. One was rich, and one was poor.* [2]*The rich man owned a great many sheep and cattle.* [3]*The poor man owned nothing but one little lamb he had bought. He raised that little lamb, and it grew up with his children. It ate from the man's own plate and drank from his cup. He cuddled it in his arms like a baby daughter.* [4]*One day a guest arrived at the home of the rich man. But instead of killing an animal from his own flock or herd, he took the poor man's lamb and killed it and prepared it for his guest."* [5]*David was furious. "As surely as the LORD lives," he vowed, "any man who would do such a thing deserves to die!* [6]*He must repay four lambs to the poor man for the one he stole and for having no pity."* [7] *Then Nathan said to David, "You are that man! The LORD, the God of Israel, says: I anointed you king of Israel and saved you from the power of Saul.* [8]*I gave you your master's house and his wives and the kingdoms of Israel and Judah. And if that had not been enough, I would have given you much, much more.* [9]*Why, then, have you despised the word of the LORD and done this horrible deed? For you have murdered Uriah the Hittite with the sword of the Ammonites and stolen his wife.* [10]*From this time on, your family will live by the sword because you have despised me by taking Uriah's wife to be your own."*

Wow, that's a lot to take in. So, what do we learn from this favorite passage? We learn that we must be aware of our own sins. We must confess, and even as David confessed and was forgiven, like David we have to accept the consequences of our actions. Forgiveness doesn't necessarily erase the consequences of a persons' actions. And here's the kicker, as God forgives us, so we are to forgive others. Even in forgiving others, there are still boundaries or consequences that may be in play – ie: abusers can be forgiven, but they do NOT have to be a part of our lives; criminals can be forgiven, but they still serve time in prison.

October 20

**<u>Psalm 27:4</u>** (NIV) *One thing I ask from the LORD, this only do I seek: that I may dwell in the house of the LORD all the days of my life, to gaze on the beauty of the LORD and to seek him in his temple.*

This favorite verse just goes straight to my heart. The Psalmist asks one thing only: "to dwell in God's house". It reminds me that, as a Christian, I have the blessing of dwelling in the house of the Lord and should savor the blessings received as a child of God. It's amazing to feel the Presence of God and be under His wings throughout life. But sometimes we do things that make Him very sad; we break His heart. Oh, He loves us through it, but as I write this it breaks my heart that I am not always presenting myself as one who lives in the house of the Lord, and dwells in His presence. Sometimes my pride comes bubbling to the surface during a disagreement, and I huff and puff like the big bad wolf. I'm working on it, and I'm grateful for a loving Father Who picks me up and dusts me off every time I fall short…

October 21

**<u>Philippians 2:9-11</u>** (NLT) [9] *Therefore, God elevated him to the place of highest honor and gave him the name above all other names,* [10] *that at the name of Jesus every knee should bow, in heaven and on earth and under the earth,* [11] *and every tongue declare that Jesus Christ is Lord, to the glory of God the Father.*

Have y'all noticed that many of my favorite verses or passages begin with the word "therefore". It ALWAYS means "because of what you just read, then the following is true". So, because of that, I looked, and the prior verses spoke of Jesus humbling Himself, becoming a man and dying on the cross. As a result of what Jesus did, God exalted Him, and I love these words of verse ten: **"at the name of Jesus every knee should bow"**. Oh, that just makes my heart sing and my soul rejoice! Like the song says: "Jesus, Jesus, there's just something about that name." Indeed, there is!

October 22

**Psalm 131** (NIV) *[1] My heart is not proud, LORD, my eyes are not haughty; I do not concern myself with great matters or things too wonderful for me. [2] But I have calmed and quieted myself, I am like a weaned child with its mother; like a weaned child I am content. [3] Israel, put your hope in the LORD both now and forevermore.*

One of the shorter chapters in the Bible, this favorite one has a powerful punch that I believe speaks to us here in the USA. As I write this, it is 2021, and our country is in a mess with so many different opinions as to how to get us out of said mess. In addition to our already troubled country, the COVID-19 pandemic hit the world and the USA with a vengeance. The major political parties within the USA can't seem to agree on anything. Hatred is running rampant through our land. The news media no longer report the news but spin their opinions instead of the hard-cold facts. It makes me grind my teeth, which irritates my TMJ. It makes my heart race and my blood pressure soar. And then, I read these verses…ah, what a reprieve from the cares of this life. Thank you, God, for giving me peace and rest in your arms, like a baby being fed by a loving mother. Thank you that you have everything under control, and my prayer is for our country and the world to place their hope in You. Can I get an amen?

October 23

**<u>2 Corinthians 12:6-9</u>** (NLT) [6]*If I wanted to boast, I would be no fool in doing so, because I would be telling the truth. But I won't do it, because I don't want anyone to give me credit beyond what they can see in my life or hear in my message,* [7]*even though I have received such wonderful revelations from God. So to keep me from becoming proud, I was given a thorn in my flesh, a messenger from Satan to torment me and keep me from becoming proud.* [8]*Three different times I begged the Lord to take it away.* [9]*Each time he said, "My grace is all you need. My power works best in weakness." So now I am glad to boast about my weaknesses, so that the power of Christ can work through me.*

In this favorite passage, Paul is writing to us about his work for God, as well as a physical issue that plagued him. He asked God three times to remove it from him, and instead God let him know that His grace was sufficient. Many of us have physical issues that we wish we didn't have. The older I get, the more physical ailments I have. I didn't even KNOW I had a meniscus until I tore mine!! This passage makes me think of ways to use my ailments for God's glory, knowing He's got this and everything in His hands. No matter what! Knowing that HIS GRACE IS SUFFICIENT. Period.

October 24

**1 Kings 8:22-23** (NIV) [22] *Then Solomon stood before the altar of the LORD in front of the whole assembly of Israel, spread out his hands toward heaven* [23] *and said: "LORD, the God of Israel, there is no God like you in heaven above or on earth below—you who keep your covenant of love with your servants who continue wholeheartedly in your way."*

This favorite passage is but a portion of the prayer Solomon prayed at the dedication of the Temple. God is faithful to keep His promises to us, and yet we, just like the Israelites before us, continue to not hold up our part in the covenant with God. Notice verse 23 reads "covenant of love" – that's it, y'all. LOVE – God so "loved the world" [see John 3:16]. We are to love God with all our heart, soul, mind, and strength; and love our neighbors as ourselves. So simple, and yet so hard because all too often we allow Satan into our hearts, and he wreaks havoc. Our focus should be on God and His love. We should view the world through God's eyes.

October 25

**James 4:7** (NIV) [7] *Submit yourselves, then, to God. Resist the devil, and he will flee from you.*

Well, isn't this a great favorite verse to follow yesterday? Submission to God and resisting the devil puts us on the path we should travel. Christ IS our salvation, and He has laid the foundation to keep us where we need to be. He is our Strength and our Song! We have nothing to fear. When things get bad, Christ is the "reset button" of our lives. He brings things into His light, which gives us a better perspective. Realizing and embracing the light of Christ is the game changer for us. Can I get a witness?

October 26

**<u>Genesis 22:9-12</u>** (NLT) *[9]When they arrived at the place where God had told him to go, Abraham built an altar and arranged the wood on it. Then he tied his son, Isaac, and laid him on the altar on top of the wood. [10]And Abraham picked up the knife to kill his son as a sacrifice. [11]At that moment the angel of the LORD called to him from heaven, "Abraham! Abraham!" "Yes," Abraham replied. "Here I am!" [12]"Don't lay a hand on the boy!" the angel said. "Do not hurt him in any way, for now I know that you truly fear God. You have not withheld from me even your son, your only son."*

Well, this is one of the troubling passages in the Bible! I almost left it out, because full disclosure, I'm not comfortable with this passage. So why is it a favorite, and why did I share it? The fact is it happened; it's a part of God's message to us. Just because I can't fathom God allowing Abraham nor Isaac the anguish of that day, doesn't mean I get to skip over the passage. I can't even imagine what Abraham was thinking as he and Isaac made their way to the sacrifice area that day. Nor can I imagine what was going through Isaac's mind. What I DO know is that God is God, and we are not. My lesson from this passage is that no matter where God leads me, He will provide a way. Bottom line y'all, is that we trust Him. Abraham did. We should. That's it.

October 27

**Psalm 139:1-4** (NLT) [1] *O LORD, you have examined my heart and know everything about me.*[2] *You know when I sit down or stand up. You know my thoughts even when I'm far away.* [3] *You see me when I travel and when I rest at home. You know everything I do.* [4] *You know what I am going to say even before I say it, LORD.*

This favorite passage reminds me that God knows EVERYTHING about me! He knows all I do and all I think even before I do it or think it. I'm an open book to Him. As a gag gift for my 30th birthday, I received a book entitled "All I Know about Childrearing". We all got a good laugh when I opened the book, and the pages were blank! It should probably scare me that God knows all about me, and that my open book to Him has page after page of all my actions past, current, and future. But you know what? It comforts me. I'm thankful for Someone Who accepts me warts and all. As the song says, "Just as I am" – indeed and amen. Y'all with me?

October 28

**<u>Ephesians 5:8-10</u>** (NLT) *[8]For once you were full of darkness, but now you have light from the Lord. So live as people of light! [9]For this light within you produces only what is good and right and true. [10]Carefully determine what pleases the Lord.*

This favorite passage says that we are the children of Light, and as such our lives should reflect the LIGHT (Jesus) in all that we do. Believe me, I know this is hard. I live in metro Atlanta, and rush hour can bring out the worst in anyone! But, trust me, with God's help you can even overcome the desire to lay in on the horn, utter an oath, or wave with a certain finger, when less-than-courteous drivers cross your path. God uses people as His angels, and for me He placed grandchildren in my life. They are wonderful governors for me, because I want to be a good example for them. I am a child of the Light; therefore, people should know that by my actions, even in Atlanta rush hour – just sayin'.

October 29

**Psalm 63:7-8** (NIV) [7] *Because you are my help, I sing in the shadow of your wings.* [8] *I cling to you; your right hand upholds me.*

I don't know about y'all, but these favorite verses comfort me so much. Life is hard, and knowing that God is holding my hand, and that I can "sing in the shadow of His wings" is a respite I do not deserve. Can y'all picture that? A mother hen holding her wings over her chicks, protecting them from everything?! God IS my strength and my help. He shelters me like a mother hen does her young. There isn't a moment in my life that God isn't Present and helping me. Peace and rest are mine in my God. Peace and rest are yours if you let Him in.

October 30

<u>**Psalm 4:6-8**</u> (MSG) *[6-7] Why is everyone hungry for more? "More, more," they say. "More, more." I have God's more-than-enough, More joy in one ordinary day [7-8] Than they get in all their shopping sprees. At day's end I'm ready for sound sleep, For you, GOD, have put my life back together.*

In this favorite passage the Psalmist reminds me that in this world we are always wanting more, and that's because nothing in the world can fill us up or complete us – only God. When we allow Him into our lives, we realize that He is MORE THAN ENOUGH. God is all that we need. He is our everything, and at the end of the day we find rest and peace. It's time we shared this with the world, y'all. It's not meant to be a secret. Come on, let's start sharing. Amen.

October 31

**<u>Proverbs 16:3</u>** (NIV) *Commit to the LORD whatever you do, and he will establish your plans.*

We aren't to worry – we ARE to TRUST God and live our lives in His will. He will help us fight whatever evil comes our way. We are to commit to Him, and even in the darkest of times we will prevail. You may say, "Oh no, Debi, that isn't true. I have illness, money issues, relationship issues, crimes committed against me – how is that prevailing?!" Two definitions of prevail are: 1) to gain ascendancy through strength or superiority; to triumph; 2) to be or become effective or effectual. So, I stand by my belief that regardless of what's happening in my life I will triumph and be effective with God at my side. This favorite verse says so. That's my story, and I'm sticking to it!

November 1

**Psalm 136:23-26** (MSG) [23-26] *God remembered us when we were down, His love never quits. Rescued us from the trampling boot, His love never quits. Takes care of everyone in time of need. His love never quits. Thank God, who did it all! His love never quits!*

On this the first day of the month in which we celebrate Thanksgiving, I wanted to begin a month-long study of verses for thankful hearts. It's been said that to create a new habit one must do it consistently for 30 days. Well as the church lady use to say, "isn't that convenient?" – November has 30 days! So, let's make a habit of thankfulness! I love the way The Message reads in this favorite passage. Over and over the Psalmist reminds us that God's love NEVER QUITS. The blessings of being remembered, rescued, taken care of – all things to be thankful for, from a God Who did/does it all!! Regardless of where we are in life, God is there, and HE NEVER QUITS. Amen, and thank You, God!

November 2

**1 Chronicles 16:7-10** (NLT) *[7]On that day David gave to Asaph and his fellow Levites this song of thanksgiving to the LORD: [8]Give thanks to the LORD and proclaim his greatness. Let the whole world know what he has done. [9]Sing to him; yes, sing his praises. Tell everyone about his wonderful deeds. [10]Exult in his holy name; rejoice, you who worship the LORD.*

This favorite passage is a beautiful reminder to not only thank God, but to also share with others what God has done for us. We should share with everyone what God means to us, not in a "preachy" way, but in an honest way. I'm talking about genuinely sharing with others what your relationship with God means to you. Including the times when God has said, 'no', and you continue to believe, trust, and follow Him anyway. Sharing what He does for us, and what He means to us, may change the path of someone's life. Make it real, y'all.

November 3

**<u>Colossians 4:2</u>** (NIV) *Devote yourselves to prayer, being watchful and thankful.*

This favorite verse is very straightforward and simple – devoting ourselves to prayer, being watchful and thankful. As we spend time with God in prayer it doesn't necessarily change our situation or the situation we're praying about; it changes US. Talking to God on a regular basis deepens our relationship with Him, and that improves our journey in the world. Knowing Him and being watchful so we're alert and recognize opportunities to serve others improves the quality of our own lives as well. And being thankful and grateful for everything makes all the difference in our character.

November 4

**Philippians 4:4-6** (NLT) *[4]Always be full of joy in the Lord. I say it again—rejoice! [5]Let everyone see that you are considerate in all you do. Remember, the Lord is coming soon. [6]Don't worry about anything; instead, pray about everything. Tell God what you need, and thank him for all he has done.*

A note in the margin of my Bible for this favorite passage is that the word "gentleness" in verse 5 means **don't be a control freak**. WOW was that a wake-up call for me back in the day when I first made that note. Many difficult situations occurred in my life, but it wasn't until 2010 that I began to understand there are things I just cannot control. God is in control, and even when we are saddened or absolutely torn apart by a situation the truth is: God is in control. Therefore, be gentle. God is near. Your situation may not change, but your heart will. Pray and be thankful as you present your requests to God.

November 5

**Colossians 2:6-7** (NIV) [6] *So then, just as you received Christ Jesus as Lord, continue to live your lives in him,* [7] *rooted and built up in him, strengthened in the faith as you were taught, and overflowing with thankfulness.*

Jesus is alive and well, and dwells within our hearts through the Holy Spirit. As we have read in other passages, God is always with us. This favorite passage reminds us that we walk away from Him, not the other way around. So as this passage says, we should live our lives in Him, rooted like a branch to a tree to receive the Strength only He can give. As we do this, our quality of life improves no matter what our circumstances are. Praise God, our cups overflow and our hearts overflow with thanksgiving to the Lord. Can I get an amen?

November 6

**<u>Psalm 95:2</u>** (NIV) *Let us come before him with thanksgiving and extol him with music and song.*

Worshipping God with music and song is one of the treasures I have as a Christian. No matter how I'm feeling or what may be going on with me, it seems that someone, somewhere has written and/or recorded a song I can listen to, play on the piano, or just read the lyrics to, that nails exactly where I am at that moment. In that regard Christian music is similar to Scripture for me as God speaks to me and touches my soul with His message. Favorite passages such as this one remind me to be thankful and to praise God with my songs. I am pulled out of my darkness and into the light and praise Him with thanksgiving for being Who. He. is.

November 7

<u>**Colossians 1:27**</u> (NIV) [1:27]*To them God has chosen to make known among the Gentiles the glorious riches of this mystery, which is Christ in you, the hope of glory.*

<u>**Colossians 3:15**</u> (NIV) [3:15] *Let the peace of Christ rule in your hearts, since as members of one body you were called to peace. And be thankful.*

My core is Jesus Christ. Realizing and tapping into that Truth keeps me focused and upright through all the drama in the world around us. These favorite verses remind me when we focus on Jesus – when I do – He lights my path and guides me in the way I should go. He keeps me centered and in tune with Him. Problems may not disappear, but they will become more manageable and we will have a Peace that passes all understanding. I'd say that's a lot to be thankful for, wouldn't y'all?

November 8

**<u>Hebrews 12:28-29</u>** (MSG) [28-29] *Do you see what we've got? An unshakable kingdom! And do you see how thankful we must be? Not only thankful, but brimming with worship, deeply reverent before God. For God is not an indifferent bystander. He's actively cleaning house, torching all that needs to burn, and he won't quit until it's all cleansed. God himself is Fire!*

As I've mentioned earlier, it's always good to read the verses prior to and after a passage to get a better understanding of the overall message. I chose The Message because it was clearer to me, and I hope to y'all. This favorite passage reminds us we are a part of the unshakable Kingdom of God! Let us rejoice and give thanks for our Lord! I envision God taking His finger and touching the unnecessary things in my life much like my dermatologist burns warts and other growths from my skin. God never gives up on us and will continue to burn off the bad if we allow Him to. Thank you, Lord, for not leaving me to my own mischief.

November 9

**2 Corinthians 9:12-15** (NLT) [12]*So two good things will result from this ministry of giving—the needs of the believers in Jerusalem will be met, and they will joyfully express their thanks to God.* [13]*As a result of your ministry, they will give glory to God. For your generosity to them and to all believers will prove that you are obedient to the Good News of Christ.* [14]*And they will pray for you with deep affection because of the overflowing grace God has given to you.* [15]*Thank God for this gift too wonderful for words!*

This favorite passage isn't just speaking about money, it's speaking about time, talents, and things. We, as people of faith, are to live the example of Christ and give of ourselves! Anything we do to help another individual on life's journey is appreciated. In addition to helping God's people and purpose, our gifts are overflowing expressions of gratitude to God for ALL we have. As verse 15 says "Thank God for this gift, too wonderful for words!" Amen and amen.

November 10

**Ephesians 5:20** (NIV) *always giving thanks to God the Father for everything, in the name of our Lord Jesus Christ.*

When I originally penned the words of this favorite verse in my journal (2011) I had not only read this passage, but I'd also received an email regarding gratitude. And if that wasn't enough, Jeri had given me a new book, One Thousand Gifts, that I'd been reading. When we embrace this verse, it gives feet and wings to our faith. I've learned to say "I don't like what I'm going through, God, but I know you'll get me through, and that along the way I'll learn something more about You and about myself." In late 2012, one of my sisters was murdered; less than two months later my daddy died; less than three months later one of my great-nephews drowned – God knew I'd need to shore up my faith, and He used devotions, emails, and books to instill this in me. Was that six-month stretch of my life easy? No. But I thank God He walked with me and my family every step of the way.

November 11

**<u>Matthew 11:25-30</u>** (NLT) [25]*At that time Jesus prayed this prayer: "O Father, Lord of heaven and earth, thank you for hiding these things from those who think themselves wise and clever and for revealing them to the childlike.* [26]*Yes, Father, it pleased you to do it this way!* [27]*"My Father has entrusted everything to me. No one truly knows the Son except the Father, and no one truly knows the Father except the Son and those to whom the Son chooses to reveal him."* [28]*Then Jesus said, "Come to me, all of you who are weary and carry heavy burdens, and I will give you rest.* [29]*Take my yoke upon you. Let me teach you, because I am humble and gentle at heart, and you will find rest for your souls.* [30]*For my yoke is easy to bear, and the burden I give you is light."*

November 11th is special to me because it is the day my daddy was born. He used to tease me and say the U.S. Government made it a holiday just for him. My daddy was a fine Christian man and gave me a foundation in faith by not only taking me to church, but also living what he believed. This is one of the many comforting passages in the Bible, and as a result, it is one of my favorites. It shows Jesus praising (thanking) God for what God had done. Jesus invites us to come to Him and get our rest. God is with us ALWAYS. He is our STRENGTH and our PEACE and our REST. No matter what is going on in our lives, no matter how bad things seem, no matter how our hearts are broken into a million pieces, God is with us. Thank Him for always being there, the One Constant in our otherwise chaotic lives. Can I get an amen?

November 12

**<u>1 Chronicles 29:10-13</u>** (NLT) [10]*Then David praised the* LORD *in the presence of the whole assembly: "O* LORD*, the God of our ancestor Israel, may you be praised forever and ever!* [11]*Yours, O* LORD*, is the greatness, the power, the glory, the victory, and the majesty. Everything in the heavens and on earth is yours, O* LORD*, and this is your kingdom. We adore you as the one who is over all things.* [12]*Wealth and honor come from you alone, for you rule over everything. Power and might are in your hand, and at your discretion people are made great and given strength.* [13]*O our God, we thank you and praise your glorious name!"**

God – not us - controls everything. Reading this favorite passage, and writing that "God controls everything" is easy. LIVING what I read and write is more difficult because, as a Type A Personality in recovery, I want to be in control. I'm sure many of you may feel the same way. What we (and when I say *we*, I mean me) need to embrace is the greatness and power of God gleaned from these verses. HE CONTROLS EVERYTHING BECAUSE HE IS THE CREATOR OF THE UNIVERSE; but He uses us in our faulty humanity to spread His Word. Realizing Who is in control, relinquishing that control to God, and living in and through His Presence allows us to be who He created us to be. When we embrace our role as His creations, and tap into His majesty, by our very lives we give thanks and praise to His Holy name and we show the world God. It might be that we are the only reflection of God that someone will see. They may never enter the doors of a church, but guess what, y'all? Believers ARE THE CHURCH! We need to conduct ourselves in a way that everyone we come in contact with knows we are children of the living God, and through us they experience His love.

[*This is only a portion of King David's prayer. The entire prayer continues through verse 19.]

November 13

**<u>1 Corinthians 1:4</u>** (NIV) *I always thank my God for you because of his grace given you in Christ Jesus.*

This favorite verse reminds me to be thankful for all the believers in my life who have shown me the way by their examples. Paul is thankful for the people of the church in Corinth just as we should be thankful for our church family. I've been a member of many churches in my life: Log Cabin Baptist and Bellevue Baptist (both in Macon, GA); Remount Baptist (North Charleston, SC); Highland Park Baptist (Hanahan, SC); Lost Mountain Baptist (Powder Springs, GA); Due West United Methodist, and Christ Lutheran, both in Marietta, GA. In all those congregations, I had amazing church families. The thing I've learned is that all of us, regardless of denomination, are the family of God. Stop and give thanks today for the many believers whom God put in your path because of how they lived their lives.

November 14

**1 Corinthians 15:57** (NIV) [57] *But thanks be to God! He gives us the victory through our Lord Jesus Christ.*

When a verse begins with "but," it's always a good idea to read what was written prior so you'll understand the context. Paul was talking about darkness, sin, death – BUT THANKS BE TO GOD. JESUS. Christ the Victor over all! This favorite verse reminds me that God is victorious over bad in life through Jesus. No matter what we face on this earth, no matter the outcome, victory is ours. Praise God Who gave His Son to reverse the curse of Eden we brought on ourselves. Thanks be to God!

November 15

**2 Corinthians 2:14** (NIV) [14] *But thanks be to God, who always leads us as captives in Christ's triumphal procession and uses us to spread the aroma of the knowledge of him everywhere.*

Here's another favorite verse that begins with that word "but". Prior to verse 14, Paul was writing about problems/issues in the church where people had disagreed, gotten their feelings hurt, hurt others – much like some of our congregations today – some things never change. God's probably shaking His head… BUT THANKS BE TO GOD, we have victory in spite of ourselves. We can overcome our differences, offer apologies, and continue to spread the Word and the fragrance of God's love to the world. Much like a smell can transport us back to a former time in our life, perhaps in a moment of spiritual aroma will transport someone back to a time when you shared your faith, and they'll go, "oh, yeah, God – Debi shared God's love with me". Just a thought….

November 16

**2 Thessalonians 1:3** (NIV) *We ought always to thank God for you, brothers and sisters, and rightly so, because your faith is growing more and more, and the love all of you have for one another is increasing.*

This favorite verse is another example of Paul expressing thankfulness for the people of the congregation. As we grow in Christ together, our love for one another grows as well. And as our love for one another grows, our love for all people grows, which opens our hearts to be servants of Christ to the world beyond our church. Thank God for your church family. Thank God for the opportunities of growth and service you have been given, as you become the hands and feet of God.

November 17

**Isaiah 51:3** (NIV) *The LORD will surely comfort Zion and will look with compassion on all her ruins; he will make her deserts like Eden, her wastelands like the garden of the LORD. Joy and gladness will be found in her, thanksgiving and the sound of singing.*

Just as God comforted Zion in this favorite verse, He continues to comfort His people today. He places in our hearts an Eden that is filled with all of His promises, love, mercy, and grace. Because of God, we have joy and gladness in our hearts and souls. We overflow in His love and peace, and we can’t help but be thankful and sing praises all the days of our lives. Thankfulness and singing touch my soul to its very core.

November 18

<u>**Mark 8:6-7**</u> (NIV) [6] *He told the crowd to sit down on the ground. When he had taken the seven loaves and given thanks, he broke them and gave them to his disciples to distribute to the people, and they did so.* [7] *They had a few small fish as well; he gave thanks for them also and told the disciples to distribute them.*

Reading this favorite passage, I just realized one of the reasons Jesus said we should have the faith of a child. Have you ever listened closely to a child's blessing? Not the standard "God is great" type blessing, but the ones they pray when we teach them to just talk to God. I've heard my grands say things like "Dear, God. Thank you for the potatoes and for the chicken and peas and iced tea." In other words, they bless every single food item on the table. SO DID JESUS! He blessed the bread; then He blessed the fish. My husband prays beautiful blessings, because they're unique and from his heart. At your next meal, remember to thank God for everything!

November 19

**<u>Psalm 107:21</u>** (NIV) *Let them give thanks to the LORD for his unfailing love and his wonderful deeds for mankind.*

Let's be honest. If we thanked God for everything, we'd be in prayer all the time because He's so good to us. Oh, wait, that's right, that's exactly what we're supposed to do! Pray without ceasing. I hear the whispers, "Okay, Debi has lost her marbles, we have jobs, we have school, we have Atlanta traffic – how can we pray without ceasing?" Well, first of all, all those reasons are great reasons to pray, just sayin'. Secondly, praying doesn't necessarily mean getting on your knees and closing your eyes. Breath prayers are amazing ways to stay in touch with God all through the day. When I was working, praying during my drive there and back was a daily thing. Praying while at work was a daily thing. Praying during my school day was a daily thing. Pray the way it works for you and God. Thank Him always, anytime, any way, like this favorite verse reminds us to do.

November 20

**Psalm 26:6b-7** (NLT) *[6]I come to your altar, O LORD, [7] singing a song of thanksgiving and telling of all your wonders.*

Different translations of the Bible speak to me in different ways. (I may have already said that a time or two.) These two favorite verses in the New Living Translation are just beautiful to me. Be vocal in your thanksgiving to God. At church, and really everywhere you go, sing His praises to the tops of your lungs. Remember, thanksgiving is an everyday/all year occurrence; not just something we do one Thursday a year in November.

November 21

**<u>Romans 6:17-18</u>** (NLT) [17] *Thank God! Once you were slaves of sin, but now you wholeheartedly obey this teaching we have given you.* [18] *Now you are free from your slavery to sin, and you have become slaves to righteous living.*

Thank God He has given us salvation to get out from under the shadow of sin. As this favorite passage reads, we are free to live in the love, peace and grace of all He has given us. So many times, we take our salvation and our lives in Christ for granted. We should never do that. Always, always thank God for ALL He has done for us. He has freed us from being slaves to sin! Now, if y'all are like me, it doesn't mean we'll never sin. What it means is our goal now is to live in Christ, and as we follow Him, we are more likely to live as He did – in love and peace. "Thank you, Lord, for making a way!"

November 22

**<u>Psalm 7:17</u>** (NIV) *I will give thanks to the LORD because of his righteousness; I will sing the praises of the name of the LORD Most High.*

In this favorite verse, David was giving thanks to God because he had protected him from Cush, a Benjaminite who was chasing him. As I reflect on this one verse it hits me that it is one that has meaning for me too, as it stands alone. There are so many things to thank God for in my life. I will thank Him and sing praise to Him. It makes me want to climb on a mountain top and just shout out to everyone the goodness of our Lord! Anyone with me?

November 23

**Psalm 9:1** (NIV) *I will give thanks to you, LORD, with all my heart; I will tell of all your wonderful deeds.*

This favorite Psalm was written by David, and, as in many of them, he is talking directly to God. A note in my Bible indicates this was a praise hymn. God created us to commune with Him, and what better way than talking and singing to Him. David, like us, made many bad choices, but through them all he knew the constant in his life was God. He felt God's love and forgiveness, he accepted the consequences of the choices he made, and he moved forward in his life. Not only did he sing hymns of thanksgiving to God, he shared what God had done for him with everyone. I'm thinking we should do the same. Can I get an amen?

November 24

**<u>1 Chronicles 16:34-35</u>** (NIV) [34] *Give thanks to the LORD, for he is good; his love endures forever.* [35] *Cry out, "Save us, God our Savior; gather us and deliver us from the nations, that we may give thanks to your holy name, and glory in your praise."*

These two favorite verses were so pertinent when first written, they were pertinent when I initially entered them into my journal in 2015, and they continue to be pertinent in 2021 as I finish this book. We should thank God with all our being for ALL He has done. We should also pray daily for our nation and the world during *this perilous time* – which I think began when Adam and Eve left Eden, just sayin'. We had it made in a beautiful garden and our great, great, great – actually, I'm not sure how many greats – but Adam and Eve messed it up! But don't blame them. Debi and Matt would have messed it up, too! And y'all would have, too. So, I offer this prayer: *Holy Father, we thank You so much for all you've done, and we are so sorry for all we've done. Please help us do our part to spread Your love throughout the world, and in doing so, make it better for everyone. Amen.*

November 25

**Psalm 100** (KJV) [1]*Make a joyful noise unto the LORD, all ye lands.* [2] *Serve the LORD with gladness: come before his presence with singing.* [3] *Know ye that the LORD he is God: it is he that hath made us, and not we ourselves; we are his people, and the sheep of his pasture.* [4] *Enter into his gates with thanksgiving, and into his courts with praise: be thankful unto him, and bless his name.* [5] *For the LORD is good; his mercy is everlasting; and his truth endureth to all generations.*

There are just some Scriptures that read beautifully from the King James Version, and this is one of them. It's one of my all-time favorites. I love the wording. Have you ever shouted a joyful noise to God? We are so prone to jump up and down and yell when our favorite team wins, so why not jump up and down and shout for joy over God! I'm ashamed to say I haven't been known to do that, and yet my family and friends will attest to my yelling and screaming when the Braves or the University of Georgia win their games. God is so good, ALL THE TIME; and He has given us so much, ALL THE TIME. We just need to start jumping up and down in praise and gratitude to God. Can I get a witness? Can I get an amen? Can I get somebody to jump up and down, happy-dance style?

November 26

**<u>Psalm 69:30</u>** (NIV) *I will praise God's name in song and glorify him with thanksgiving.*

Being a musician, it's easy to see why this is a favorite verse. I've been singing praise songs ever since I was a small child in Vacation Bible School and Sunday School at Log Cabin Baptist Church in Macon, GA. (There are some very old, silent, home movies to prove this.) Every time we participate in singing at church, or just singing gospel songs in the car or shower, we are praising God with our song!! The energy we bring to our songs, not only praises God, it also lifts us, and those who hear us, up. I honestly believe all Heaven joins in as well, and there is a huge sing-along as we rock the House praising God and singing our Thanksgiving.

November 27

**Psalm 147:7** (NIV) *Sing to the LORD with grateful praise; make music to our God on the harp.*

Well, I don't have a harp, although my friend, Mandy, plays one beautifully. King David DID have a harp, and his point in this favorite verse is ***use what you have to praise God***! I have a piano, and some might say "it doesn't sound like praise", but when I play hymns and gospel songs while I am communing with my God, He is one proud Papa. He created us to commune with Him. God provides all our needs, and we sometimes take that, and Him, for granted. Stop today and truly thank God for ALL He has done for you and your family. It's liable to take the whole day, but dust off your instrument, even if it's your voice, and play/sing for your proud Papa.

November 28

**Jeremiah 33:10-11** (NLT) [10]*"This is what the LORD says: You have said, 'This is a desolate land where people and animals have all disappeared.' Yet in the empty streets of Jerusalem and Judah's other towns, there will be heard once more* [11]*the sounds of joy and laughter. The joyful voices of bridegrooms and brides will be heard again, along with the joyous songs of people bringing thanksgiving offerings to the LORD. They will sing, 'Give thanks to the LORD of Heaven's Armies, for the LORD is good. His faithful love endures forever!' For I will restore the prosperity of this land to what it was in the past, says the LORD."*

The earlier verses in this chapter are about the restoration of Jerusalem. This favorite passage is God speaking through the prophet, Jeremiah. As I read these verses, I couldn't help but think of my hometown, Hanahan, SC, after hurricane Hugo hit in 1989. The devastation was mind-boggling. It looked as if a bomb had been dropped. Seeing it was like someone punching me in the stomach. I'm pretty sure the Israelites felt something similar when they saw the devastation of their beautiful city. The verses above declare that, in spite of all the bad, there will be thanksgiving as God brings healing. He did it for Jerusalem. He did it for Hanahan. He will ALWAYS do it for us. Can I get an amen?

November 29

**<u>1 Thessalonians 5:18</u>** (NIV) *give thanks in all circumstances; for this is God's will for you in Christ Jesus.*

As I read through and reviewed my devotional journals to write this book, I inevitably ran across days of deep sorrow in my life. This verse was my devotion on October 7, 2012, the day after we learned my sister, Gail, had been found dead. At that time, it had not been confirmed that she had been murdered. This is also one of the verses that I mentioned in the introduction, that may appear more than once in this book (see March 24th). I truly believe it's because God wants me to embrace and "get" this verse. He wants me to share it with y'all. Life isn't fair. Life isn't easy. There are times we just don't *<u>feel</u>* thankful – we don't feel anything. God knows that, and He wants us to know that **even in those times He's with us**, walking beside us or maybe even carrying us. And for Him and His Presence, we can be thankful.

November 30

**<u>Daniel 2:23</u>** (NIV) *I thank and praise you, God of my ancestors: You have given me wisdom and power, you have made known to me what we asked of you, you have made known to us the dream of the king.*

The history behind this favorite verse is King Nebuchadnezzar had a dream that none of the palace magicians, enchanters, sorcerers or astrologers could interpret. Daniel and his friends prayed for wisdom to interpret the dream, and God allowed them the knowledge to do so. Verse 23 is Daniel's prayer thanking God for giving him and his friends the wisdom they needed. So many times we pray for one thing or another, but we are sometimes not so quick to thank God afterward. Give thanks always. God is so good; how could we not thank Him?

December 1

**Isaiah 9:6** (NIV) *For to us a child is born, to us a son is given, and the government will be on his shoulders. And he will be called Wonderful Counselor, Mighty God,*
*Everlasting Father, Prince of Peace.*

This favorite verse is not only the prophecy of Christ's birth, but also the prophecy of His triumphant entry into Jerusalem. The words of this verse have always spoken directly to my heart. The majesty and the excitement in these verses fill me with anticipation, love, and peace. They prepare me for the Christmas season approaching, knowing that His cradle was always in the shadow of His cross. They remind me of the beautiful life He led, as an example to all of us.

December 2

**Colossians 3:14-15** (NLT) [14] *Above all, clothe yourselves with love, which binds us all together in perfect harmony.* [15] *And let the peace that comes from Christ rule in your hearts. For as members of one body you are called to live in peace. And always be thankful.*

Prior to these favorite verses, Paul had been writing about putting aside their feelings/actions of hurt, anger, immorality, bitterness, hatefulness, etc. that they had before Christ, and embracing the fruits of the Spirit they have in their new life in Christ: compassion, kindness, humility, gentleness, patience, forgiveness (as God forgave us). Guess what, y'all. This is STILL TRUE. It is so hard to forgive* people who don't deserve it. That's called mercy, and I struggle with it to this day. I'm not sharing anything with y'all I don't need to hear myself. Above ALL the virtues listed above is that four-letter word that carries such force: ***LOVE***. That is God's story in a nutshell. And then peace, His peace, will rule our hearts. If the body of Christ can just get it right, we can change the world. Can I get a witness!?

*I must stop here and say that forgiveness doesn't mean the person(s) who caused you pain gets a pass. No, the consequences, whatever they may be, are still there. But your heart is not weighed down, or blemished, because of an unforgiving spirit. I speak as someone who through Christ forgave the people who murdered her sister. They are all in prison where they belong. I speak as someone who has suffered abuse in my past. The abusers don't get to be a part of my life, but I have forgiven them. I hope y'all get what I mean here.

December 3

**James 4:13-15** (NLT) [13] *Look here, you who say, "Today or tomorrow we are going to a certain town and will stay there a year. We will do business there and make a profit."* [14] *How do you know what your life will be like tomorrow? Your life is like the morning fog—it's here a little while, then it's gone.* [15] *What you ought to say is, "If the Lord wants us to, we will live and do this or that."*

In this favorite passage, James is reminding us that God is God and we are not. We can't just go our merry way making plans that don't include God! If He's a part of our very being, how ridiculous is it that we leave Him out!? I mean, really. Think about it. We either have Him in our lives, or we don't. And if we do, then for goodness sake involve Him in our plans! There are verses all throughout Scripture stating that God will guide us. Well, He can't guide us if we're running ahead of Him. Just sayin'. Trust God with ALL your desires, plans, dreams. I guarantee He will ALWAYS be there for you and me!

December 4

**Deuteronomy 4:29** (NIV) *But if from there you seek the LORD your God, you will find him if you seek him with all your heart and with all your soul.*

First of all, let me say I really like December 4th because that's the day I became a mom! Shout out, to Jeri – Happy Birthday! And now, back to the book: The setting of the above favorite verse is Moses telling the Israelites that when they are scattered among nations that don't serve God, they can still seek and find Him. The same holds true for us today, whether it be at work, at school, on the subway, anywhere we are, God is there too! If we seek God with all our heart and soul, we will find Him – that's a promise, and God doesn't break promises.

December 5

**<u>Genesis 3:8-9</u>** (NLT) [8]*When the cool evening breezes were blowing, the man and his wife heard the LORD God walking about in the garden. So they hid from the LORD God among the trees.* [9]*Then the LORD God called to the man, "Where are you?"*

Many times, we try to hide from God just as Adam and Eve did after they had eaten the forbidden fruit and messed up the Garden of Eden for all of us – otherwise known as "the fall". Y'all may be wondering why in the world this is a favorite passage. Well, it's because it explains why sin is in the world, and why God loves us still. First of all, God knew where they were, He just wanted them to own where they were, and examine their own hearts. Secondly, don't be too hard on them, because something tells me none of us would have withstood the temptation either. Wouldn't have mattered if it were Debi and Matt Merchant, or Mickey and Minnie Mouse – the fall would have happened because God gave us free will. Without God in our lives, we can't handle free will. And, full disclosure, even with God in my life, I repeatedly fumble the free will aspect of my life. We can't hide from God. He knows exactly where we are in our walk with Him. Allow Him to walk with you and guide you. And when you (I) stumble, own it!

December 6

**<u>2 Corinthians 6:10</u>** (NIV) *sorrowful, yet always rejoicing; poor, yet making many rich; having nothing, and yet possessing everything.*

This favorite verse is actually describing Paul and the other missionaries of the first century, but it resonates with me so much. I am blessed beyond my comprehension; He is ALL I NEED. Just as the words to the old hymn says "and He walks with me and He talks with me" – He does! And there is nothing on earth that compares with that! No matter what happens to me, I grab hold of His nailed-scarred hand and Peace floods my soul. I crawl into His lap, and as an earthly parent comforts their child, my Lord comforts me. With God, I possess everything.

.

December 7

**<u>John 15:5</u>** (NIV) *I am the vine; you are the branches. If you remain in me and I in you, you will bear much fruit; apart from me you can do nothing.*

Jesus is speaking in this favorite verse. He's talking to you and He's talking to me. I know that apart from Christ, I am nothing. He is my Strength. I am created in His image to commune with Him. When I initially wrote this verse in my journal, it was September 2012. I'm not sure now what was going on with me then, but here is what I wrote: *I am troubled this morning so I'm up much earlier than I need to be and it's because the only way for me to find peace is to be with God right now. And who knew but Him, that this would be the verse I would read and how it would calm my spirit. Thank you, Father.* Isn't it a comfort that God knows exactly what we need, when we need it? AND He takes us right to it! May this verse also speak to your soul.

December 8

**Isaiah 26:4** (NIV) *Trust in the LORD forever, for the LORD, the Lord himself, is the Rock eternal.*

Well, that verse sums it up nicely, don't you think? No wonder it's a favorite verse of mine. Trust in God for everything!! As I write this, our beautiful, old hound dog, Tucker, is at the vet, and we may be receiving bad news when we pick him up later today. I had no idea that this would be the next verse from my journals, but God knew. And this is His way of telling me no matter what, He's got this. He's got Tucker in His hands. EVERYTHING includes all that is important to us, even an old hound dog. So, I'm wiping my tears away, and I'm trusting in God to guide us and lead us in whatever the case may be. Our understanding is limited, but God is all knowing.

December 9

**<u>Isaiah 54:10</u>** (NIV) *"Though the mountains be shaken and the hills be removed, yet my unfailing love for you will not be shaken nor my covenant of peace be removed," says the* L*ORD, who has compassion on you.*

Praise God for His love for us. I love this favorite verse because it clearly states that God's love is unfailing and unshakable. All of the earth will pass away, but not God's love for us! Not His peace, not His kindness. He has promised to be with us and keep us in all places – even the end of the world. So those who are afraid of the end of the world, and run off to hide in caves, etc. – I say to them, "God has this. Y'all can just relax and live your lives."

(Tucker update: X-rays and bloodwork showed Tucker is in good shape for his age, and the issue he's having can most likely be handled with steroids and antibiotic. What a relief!)

December 10

**<u>Matthew 7:1</u>** (NIV) *Do not judge, or you too will be judged.*

Jesus is speaking in this favorite verse. If y'all are as old as I am, you might remember this verse reading something like "judge not that ye be not judged by the same measure". That's because the King James version (KJV) contained those words. I went online to see why those words were removed, and I got more confused than ever, so this is going to be the *interpretation of Debi version* of this verse. The "same measure" of the KJV meant "human eye/ intellect" are limited and we can't see or know the big picture, or the hearts of individuals. Only God can see and do that. So, it's simple – you don't know the whole story, ergo, don't judge. Got it? Good.

December 11

**Mark 8:36** (NIV) *What good is it for someone to gain the whole world, yet forfeit their soul?*

We run here and there chasing rainbows and wanting success in life. What does that gain us if we leave God out of our equation? In this favorite verse, Jesus reminds me nothing is anything without God. He has known us before we were born. Scripture tells us, “He knit us in our mother’s womb” (see Psalm 139:13). How can we leave Him out? I really don’t get it. If He knit us, then He is part of us, and when we run around trying to fill a void that won’t be filled, it’s because only HE can fill that void. Don’t give up God for something fleeting and passing. Anyone want to shout an amen?

December 12

**1 John 2:15-17** (NIV) [15] *Do not love this world nor the things it offers you, for when you love the world, you do not have the love of the Father in you.* [16] *For the world offers only a craving for physical pleasure, a craving for everything we see, and pride in our achievements and possessions. These are not from the Father, but are from this world.* [17] *And this world is fading away, along with everything that people crave. But anyone who does what pleases God will live forever.*

This favorite passage today reminds us to have our eyes set on God and the things of God, not the things of the world. We in Christ are set apart, and as such we should live in a way that no one should have to ask if we are Christians or be surprised to find out that we are. Things of the world are temporary, but the things of God are eternal. God's will for our lives will be so much better than anything we could possibly imagine! As we align ourselves with His will, love, life and peace will fill our hearts.

December 13

**Proverbs 20:24** (MSG) *The very steps we take come from God; otherwise how would we know where we're going?*

This favorite verse explains my life! Without God leading me, I'd have no idea where to go or how to get there. Walking with God does NOT mean I'm perfect. FAR FROM IT! I stumble every day; some who know me well would say every hour. This verse lets us know how much He cares for us, and there's not a step we take that He doesn't know about. He's there for us always, we just have to invite Him along.

December 14

**1 Kings 19:12** (NIV) *After the earthquake came a fire, but the LORD was not in the fire. And after the fire came a gentle whisper.*

This favorite verse reminds me that God doesn't scream and holler, nor does He jump up and down and have a hissy fit*. In the verse preceding this one, God had not been in the wind or the earthquake. He doesn't make a splash to get our attention. I think that's because He wants us listening and watching for Him. When He's quiet, we have to pay close attention – and that is the key. That gentle whisper is life-changing.

**[It's a Southern thing.]*

December 15

**Genesis 37-47** (NLT) [4] *"Please, come closer," he said to them. So they came closer. And he said again, "I am Joseph, your brother, whom you sold into slavery in Egypt.* [5] *But don't be upset, and don't be angry with yourselves for selling me to this place. It was God who sent me here ahead of you to preserve your lives."* (from Chapter 45)

Okay, don't have a cow, you don't ***have*** to read these ten chapters in Genesis. However, if you were to, what a story! Just sayin'. It's a favorite of mine, and it all boils down to the two verses listed above. Joseph always held onto his faith, and he knew it had been God's will all along for him to end up in Egypt prior to the famine. Even through the hardships and unfair treatment he received, Joseph remained true to God and God blessed him. In spite of what his brothers did to him, he loved them. The lesson is to keep our faith through it all, and God will be our Person through it all.

December 16

**<u>Psalm 68:19</u>** (NIV) *Praise be to the Lord, to God our Savior, who daily bears our burdens.*

When I first entered this favorite verse into my journal, it was September 23, 2012, and I was sitting on the deck of the Delta Queen steamboat, now a hotel, moored on the Tennessee River in Chattanooga, TN. I was having my morning coffee with God. Being on that deck overlooking the river each morning had been a very moving experience for me. This day was even more special as a lady walked passed me, stopped, and ask me to read her a verse. I read her the above verse, and two strangers – yet sisters in Christ – shared a brief moment together sharing how our God bears our burdens. Little did I know that less than two weeks later our family would suffer a catastrophic event, and we'd all cling to God bearing our burden!

December 17

**<u>Hebrews 10:23</u>** (NIV) *Let us hold unswervingly to the hope we profess, for he who promised is faithful.*

This favorite verse reminds me to put out of my heart and mind all the things that separate me from my relationship with God. He is faithful and will fulfill ALL His promises to us. We need to hold fast to Who and what we know, remembering Whose we are and basking in His unconditional love for us. So many things in life pull us away from God, and into different directions. Take a hold of His hand, and don't allow yourself to lose focus.

December 18

**2 Peter 1:2** (NIV) *Grace and peace be yours in abundance through the knowledge of God and of Jesus our Lord.*

We are so blessed when we walk with Christ. We know the sound of His voice and hear Him as we commune together. Keeping our eyes focused on Him and allowing Him to guide us on our path, makes all the difference in the world to the journey we take. Grace, peace, and love will ALWAYS be with us as we walk and talk with our God. This favorite verse assures us of that. Can I get a witness?

December 19

**Psalm 23:4** (NIV) *Even though I walk through the darkest valley, I will fear no evil, for you are with me; your rod and your staff, they comfort me.*

Psalm 23 is one of my very favorite passages. The above verse speaks of the lowest point in our lives. No matter where I walk in this life – even the **darkest valley** (death, or a metaphor for a horrible situation) – God is with me and will comfort and protect me. I have a note in my Bible margin that emphasizes walk – not camp out – in the darkness. At 68, I've been through and seen some horrible times in my life, and not once has fear or worry helped me through. ONLY GOD, ONLY GOD. God has NEVER let me down. God has NEVER left me alone. God has always been there, and in many times carried me. No need to fear anything when our Father is God.

December 20

**<u>Matthew 27:50-51</u>** <u>(NLT)</u> [50] *Then Jesus shouted out again, and he released his spirit.* [51] *At that moment the curtain in the sanctuary of the Temple was torn in two, from top to bottom. The earth shook, rocks split apart,* [52] *and tombs opened. The bodies of many godly men and women who had died were raised from the dead.*

You may wonder why, as we near Christmas, I include verses from the Crucifixion. Well, it's to remind us that's why He came to earth. These favorite verses recount how He reconciled us to have a "one-on-one" relationship with God. No more curtains. That's why He walked among us. We truly can't think of the cradle without also thinking of the cross. Every Christmas, we not only light up a nativity in our yard, but we also have a cross casting it's shadow on the cradle. Indeed, Jesus knew that He walked in the shadow of the cross. Because He did, we can live in the shadow of that cross where He bore all our sin. Where He became sin for us. And at the moment He died, as the verse above says, there is no longer a curtain separating us from God. We can all enter into His Presence. We can thank our Lord, for His cradle with a cross.

December 21

**Deuteronomy 33:27** (NIV) *The eternal God is your refuge, and underneath are the everlasting arms. He will drive out your enemies before you, saying, 'Destroy them!'*

Isn't it wonderful that God is our refuge and our strength? Isn't it wonderful that His everlasting arms hold us up as we navigate all the pitfalls and disappointments of this life? This favorite verse is so clear about this. He gives us strength and confidence to keep moving against all odds. He carries us when we can no longer walk. He drives out our enemies, whether physical or inside our heads. He furnishes us with the tools to overcome. Though the world be dark, we focus on God and see His Light shining on everything! He IS our Refuge. His everlasting arms hold and carry us. He does destroy our enemies. Can I get an amen?

December 22

**John 8:58** (NIV) *"Very truly I tell you," Jesus answered, "before Abraham was born, I am!"*

I love how Jesus always had an answer. In this favorite verse, Jesus is answering the religious leaders of the day, as they are trying to catch Him in a lie and discredit what He is saying. When Moses asked God what name he should use for God, God replied, "I AM WHO I AM." (Exodus 3:14) (NIV). Jesus is referencing that in this verse, and declaring that He is God, and has been God from the beginning. The book of Genesis references "let **us** make mankind in **our** image" (Genesis 1:26a)(NIV), and the book of John references Jesus has been here from the beginning of time (John 1:1-5). The Plan for Him to come and dwell among us as old as mankind, because, guess what? God knew we'd mess up in the Garden. Just sayin'.

December 23

**Psalm 13:5** (NIV) *But I trust in your unfailing love; my heart rejoices in your salvation.*

This favorite verse reminds me not only of God's unfailing love, but also of His salvation. He loved us enough to save us from ourselves. God is Sovereign and we are to trust Him no matter what – even when it seems we are spiraling out of control. We place our hands into His hands, and our lives into His arms, and the most amazing peace envelops us. The most amazing strength takes hold, when two seconds earlier you felt you couldn't take even one step forward. Give thanks that no matter the situation "God's got your back". Always!

December 24

**<u>Luke 2:1-7</u>** (NLT) [1]*At that time the Roman emperor, Augustus, decreed that a census should be taken throughout the Roman Empire.* [2]*(This was the first census taken when Quirinius was governor of Syria.)* [3]*All returned to their own ancestral towns to register for this census.* [4]*And because Joseph was a descendant of King David, he had to go to Bethlehem in Judea, David's ancient home. He traveled there from the village of Nazareth in Galilee.* [5]*He took with him Mary, his fiancée, who was now obviously pregnant.* [6]*And while they were there, the time came for her baby to be born.* [7]*She gave birth to her first child, a son. She wrapped him snugly in strips of cloth and laid him in a manger, because there was no lodging available for them.*

For some reason I chose to read this favorite passage aloud, and as I did my dogs lay quietly as if listening. God was here. With. Me. And. My. Dogs. We are never alone even when we feel or think that we are. I'm convinced my dogs felt His Presence. I know, y'all may think me silly, but that doesn't change my mind. God was right here. As an aside, dog spelled backward is God, and I don't think that's an accident because both God and dogs love unconditionally. And He is here with us today, just as clearly as when He arrived on this earth as a baby on that first Christmas. To me this passage is the first half of one of the most beautiful passages in the Bible.

December 25

**<u>Luke 2:8-20</u>** (NLT) *[8]That night there were shepherds staying in the fields nearby, guarding their flocks of sheep. [9]Suddenly, an angel of the Lord appeared among them, and the radiance of the Lord's glory surrounded them. They were terrified, [10]but the angel reassured them. "Don't be afraid!" he said. "I bring you good news that will bring great joy to all people. [11]The Savior—yes, the Messiah, the Lord—has been born today in Bethlehem, the city of David! [12]And you will recognize him by this sign: You will find a baby wrapped snugly in strips of cloth, lying in a manger." [13]Suddenly, the angel was joined by a vast host of others—the armies of heaven—praising God and saying, [14]"Glory to God in highest heaven, and peace on earth to those with whom God is pleased." [15]When the angels had returned to heaven, the shepherds said to each other, "Let's go to Bethlehem! Let's see this thing that has happened, which the Lord has told us about." [16]They hurried to the village and found Mary and Joseph. And there was the baby, lying in the manger. [17]After seeing him, the shepherds told everyone what had happened and what the angel had said to them about this child. [18]All who heard the shepherds' story were astonished, [19]but Mary kept all these things in her heart and thought about them often. [20]The shepherds went back to their flocks, glorifying and praising God for all they had heard and seen. It was just as the angel had told them.*

My husband and I had the privilege of visiting the Holy Land in March 2019. We walked where Jesus walked. We saw the place the Church has long thought to be where Mary first laid her Son in a manger. It was really a cave, not a stable as most of us grew up thinking. We also visited Shepherd's Field, where the shepherds kept their flocks on that long-ago night. I wish my words could adequately describe how I felt standing there. The awe and wonder of it all! Shepherds were the lowest on the totem pole, so to speak, and yet God chose them to be the first to hear the good news. Clearly letting the world know His Son was for all of us! And those humble men did just what the angels told them to do. They met the Christ Child, and then they told the world. We who have met the Christ Child should do the same. Tell the world how the Christ Child has changed your life. This is the second half of one of the most beautiful passages in the Bible. Merry Christmas, y'all!

December 26

**<u>1 Peter 1:14-17</u>** (MSG) *As obedient children, let yourselves be pulled into a way of life shaped by God's life, a life energetic and blazing with holiness. God said, "I am holy; you be holy." You call out to God for help and he helps—he's a good Father that way. But don't forget, he's also a responsible Father, and won't let you get by with sloppy living.*

God came to earth to show us how to live, plain and simple. In that living we accept His gift of Salvation, and we abide in Him. These favorite verses touch the depths of my soul. I so often screw up my life and just make a mess of things because I fail to include God in the equation of my life. If we (I) live as Christ lived we are (I am) allowing God to shape our lives (my life) by His life. *Energetic, blazing with holiness.* Doesn't that excite y'all? God said: "I AM holy; you be holy." Oh, that just gives me chills!!! Allow God to mold you into who He created you to be. Lean on Him. He won't let us be sloppy if we're in His Word. Can I get an amen?

December 27

**<u>Romans 5:2b-5</u>** (NLT) [2]*Because of our faith, Christ has brought us into this place of undeserved privilege where we now stand, and we confidently and joyfully look forward to sharing God's glory.* [3]*We can rejoice, too, when we run into problems and trials, for we know that they help us develop endurance.* [4]*And endurance develops strength of character, and character strengthens our confident hope of salvation.* [5]*And this hope will not lead to disappointment. For we know how dearly God loves us, because he has given us the Holy Spirit to fill our hearts with his love.*

All righty, this favorite passage pretty much describes my life; how about yours? The only thing I have to boast about is my God, my Lord, my Savior. Without God, I am nothing. He's the fiber of my being. Suffering is a part of life, and just because God is also a part of life, He doesn't erase the suffering – He helps us through it. He gives us strength. He gives us power. And all along the sufferings of this life mold our character and shape us into who God created us to be. His children, seeking Him and walking with Him always.

December 28

**<u>Matthew 6:34</u>** (NIV) *Therefore do not worry about tomorrow, for tomorrow will worry about itself. Each day has enough trouble of its own.*

Don't you hate it when you let the little things in life take on a life of their own, and the molehills become mountains? I do that occasionally; not as much now as when I was younger, but I do still catch myself wandering into that murky area. Why? Logically (Mr. Spock just popped into my head, Captain), it makes no sense. Worry can't change a thing except perhaps raise your blood pressure and cause other health issues. So why worry? I'm thankful in my "mature" years, that I hear God whispering, "Debi, I've got this," when I feel the worry-wart in me rear its ugly head. Praise God, He DOES have this. He spoke this favorite verse long ago, and Matthew wrote it down. God knew that one day you and I would read it. Someone shout "AMEN"!

December 29

**Luke 12:7** (NIV) *Indeed, the very hairs of your head are all numbered. Don't be afraid; you are worth more than many sparrows.*

Jesus spoke these words. This favorite verse makes the hairs on my arms and the back of my neck stand straight up. Really! Praise God for the love He has for us. Even the hairs on our heads are numbered! Good grief, y'all, if God knows how many hairs are on our heads, then surely to goodness, He's got us in His hands and will take care of us. Don't you think? Every day should be lived in happiness and joy in the Lord! We have so much to be thankful for. Even in our darkest, scariest days… GOD! Always and only, God. Amen.

December 30

**John 14:16-17** (NLT) [16] *And I will ask the Father, and he will give you another Advocate, who will never leave you.* [17] *He is the Holy Spirit, who leads into all truth. The world cannot receive him, because it isn't looking for him and doesn't recognize him. But you know him, because he lives with you now and later will be in you.*

In this favorite passage, Jesus was telling the disciples and us, that He would send the Holy Spirit to be with us once He was no longer physically on the earth. The reason I know this is because Jesus said it! The Holy Spirit is how God lives within us. It's how we ALL have God all the time. Our power is from the Spirit. God, the THREE in ONE! Father – Creator God; Son – Jesus Christ; Mother – Holy Spirit/Comforter/Counselor. "I will never leave you nor abandon you" (Hebrews 13:5) (CSB) – and He never has. Praise God!

December 31

**Habakkuk 3:17-*19*** (NLT) [17] *Even though the fig trees have no blossoms, and there are no grapes on the vines; even though the olive crop fails, and the fields lie empty and barren; even though the flocks die in the fields, and the cattle barns are empty,* [18] *yet I will rejoice in the* LORD*! I will be joyful in the God of my salvation!* [19] *The Sovereign* LORD *is my strength! He makes me as surefooted as a deer, able to tread upon the heights.*

In this favorite passage, the prophet, Habakkuk, listed many of the horrible things that could go wrong back in his day. Yet, he said "I will rejoice in the Lord." On this the last day of the year, let us remember, that rejoicing in the Lord has nothing to do with our circumstances, and everything to do with our hearts. Trust, faith, love in God leads to strength, joy, and peace in our lives. May the coming year find you and yours at peace, knowing your Heavenly Father has your back, no matter what. Sing a hymn to God, and dance in His love. Happy New Year, y'all!

**Acknowledgements**

There are so many people to thank. This truly has been a journey in which many family members and friends have shared.

First, and foremost, my husband, Matthew, who has always encouraged my "writing bug". From the very beginning of our relationship, he saw something in me that I didn't see in myself. In 2005, he enrolled me into a Saturday class at Emory University (his employer) entitled Write Your First Book in 52 Weeks or Less. That day changed my life. It put into me the fire I needed to embrace my love of the written word and it ignited the author within. For the first time in my life, I *felt* like a writer. As writing became my reality, he kept the house running while I chased my dream. He always has encouraging words for me. Matthew, I could NOT have done this without you. I love you forever and always.

Secondly, Jeri Michelle, the woman who made me a mom, and the woman who asked for a list of my favorite Scriptures. Without that request, there surely would never have been this book. At the time, I emailed you a long list of my favorite Bible verses, but I neglected to explain why they were favorites. So this book is your complete answer. Thank you, Jeri, for wanting to grow in your own Spiritual journey, and wanting to understand mine.

Now, in no particular order, I thank the following:

Paul Davis (a retired minister) and Ann Mann (currently a minister) were my "spiritual barometers" in this journey. Jeri, Kathy Dover (my sister), Debra Brumley and Deb Christmas (both dear friends) each read portions of my manuscript. All of these people offered sage advice along the way.

Susan Shaneyfelt, and Susie Taylor (both dear friends) each read the proof.

My artist, and dear fried, Annette Langevin Lewis, listened carefully to my vision and created the perfect cover for my book. If you're in need of an artist, contact her at annetteportfolio.weebly.com or annettelangevinlewisart on Instagram.

FoxTale Book Shoppe is my happy place, an amazing eclectic bookstore in Woodstock, GA, that also offers writing courses. I've had the privilege of attending courses there since 2014. COVID19 stopped the in-person courses for a while, but the courses continued using the technology available through Zoom, Hangout, and others. From those courses grew an amazing writing group of which I'm forever grateful to be a participant. Crystal, Gretchen, Angie, Ira, Evie, Suzanne, Jennifer, Linda, Heather, Michele, and Lisa – thank you all for your input and friendship in our journeys to become comfortable with our written words.

And last, but not least, Beth Hermes who has been my writing coach since I began classes at the book shoppe. Beth is not only my coach, but she is also a dear friend, my editor, and my publisher. Your ability to see your students' potential and say just the right thing to make the spark a roaring fire is a gift. I'm blessed to have met you and have you in my life. Thank you, so much.

**[Author's Note: I realize there are errors in this book, and trust me, my proofreaders found and noted them. I am authentically imperfect and chose to leave some errors that are uniquely me. Welcome to my world.]*

## About the Author

Although she was born in Georgia, Debi Barrington Merchant grew up in a small town outside of Charleston, South Carolina.

She jokingly says she's been "in church" since she was two weeks old. She accepted Christ as her Savior when she was six years old, and while she has no huge salvation story, she certainly has stories of the staying power of her faith.

She caught the writing bug at age 13, and penned her first "book," *All's Well That Ends Well*, that same year.

Putting aside her dreams of being a writer when "real life" got in the way she began a 34-plus-year run as a civilian employee for the U.S. Government. Now retired, she has become the author she always dreamed of being.

You can read more about Debi on her website: www.debiwithani.com.

Debi is married to Matthew Merchant, and lives outside Atlanta, Georgia.

Made in the USA
Columbia, SC
14 January 2022